MARKETING OF SERVICES
A STUDY

MARKETING OF SERVICES
A STUDY

Dr. Mushtaq Bhat

ANMOL PUBLICATIONS PVT. LTD.
NEW DELHI - 110 002 (INDIA)

ANMOL PUBLICATIONS PVT. LTD.
H.O.: 4374/4B, Ansari Road, Darya Ganj,
New Delhi-110 002 (India)
Ph.: 23261597, 23278000

B.O.: No. 1015, Ist Main Road, BSK IIIrd Stage
IIIrd Phase, IIIrd Block,
Bangalore - 560 085 (India)
Visit us at: www.anmolpublications.com

Marketing of Services a Study

First Published, 2006

ISBN 81-261-2696-5

PRINTED IN INDIA

Published by J.L. Kumar for Anmol Publications Pvt. Ltd., New Delhi - 110 002 and Printed at Mehra Offset Press, Delhi.

Contents

Acknowledgements

During the course of research, I feel lucky to have received guidance, help, comments and criticism from many quarters. I deem it my pleasure to acknowledge with gratitude all of them here. If, I miss any or some of them to mention by name, it would be my absent mindedness but certainly not intentional.

First of all, I feel great pleasure in expressing my profound sense of gratitude to my respected and learned supervisor Prof. Sayyed Fayyaz Ahmad, Head, Department of Commerce, University of Kashmir, for his able guidance and supervision. In spite of his busy schedule, he took keen interest in the completion of this work. Without his encouragement, inspiration, healthy suggestions and constructive criticism, this project would have hardly been completed.

I am equally indebted to my venerable co-supervisor, Dr. Abdul Gani, Regional Director, IGNOU, Srinagar, who, in spite of his busy academic and administrative engagements, has been a constant source of inspiration, comfort, moral support and encouragement through every phase of the present research endeavor. He and all the members of his family always treated me as part of their family. I once again wish to acknowledge my gratitude to all of them for their support and blessings to the project.

I shall be failing my duty if I do not place on record my thanks to my maternal uncle, Prof. A. S. Bhat, Dean Academics,

University of Kashmir, for his moral support, encouragement and keen interest in the completion of present research project. I acknowledge my sincere regards and gratitude to him and members of his family for their support and encouragement.

I concede that whatever is really appreciable in this study is a result of my constant interaction with some eminent academic personalities and practitioners. I express my unrestrained gratitude to all of them for their scholarly discussions, comments, suggestions and supply of valuable literature. In particular, I am grateful to Prof. M.L. Aggarwal, (Coordinator, Center for Services Management, XLRI, Jamshedpur), Prof. Vijay Mahajan (University of Texas, USA), Prof. Sunjay K. Jain (Delhi School of Economics, University of Delhi), Prof. D.P.S. Verma (Delhi School of Economics, University of Delhi), Prof. S.P. Gupta (Head and Dean, FIMS, University of Delhi), and Dr. Sami A. Khan (Institute for Integrated Learning in Management, Delhi) from whose research experiences I have enormously gained and who have alerted me to all such sources that matter in the field of services marketing. I also acknowledge my indebtedness to all those practitioners whose practical experience and scholarly discussions contributed in the completion of this research project. In particular I am thankful to Mr. M. Altaf (Branch Manager, J&K Bank, Hazratbal, Srinagar), Mr. P.K. Puri (Branch Manager, SBI, East Patel Nagar, New Delhi), Mr. I.J. Khattar (Training Manager, PNB, Ludhiana), Mr. Y.K. Sharma (Branch Manager, SBI, Chandigarh) and Mr. A.G. Labroo (Branch Manager, SBI, Anantnag) for their fruitful discussions and valuable suggestions. I shall be failing in my duty if I do not place on record my sincere and grateful thanks to all those authors and writers, in India and abroad, from whose writings I have been benefited.

I acknowledge my indebtedness to all those bank officers and bank customers, whom I interviewed during my field survey, for their whole hearted and active cooperation, without which it would not have been possible to complete the survey, which forms the basis of the present work.

I am grateful to the officials of Council for Social Development, New Delhi, for the computer analysis work without which it would have been difficult to complete the present research work. I acknowledge my deep indebtedness to Mr. Bashir Ahmad Bhat, Population Research Center, University of Kashmir, for his unqualified help for the data analysis. I am grateful to him for his personal interest and help in the form of fruitful discussions and scholarly criticisms as far as application of statistical tools are concerned.

All my colleagues in the Department of Commerce, University of Kashmir, Srinagar have contributed to the completion of this project by way of their cooperation and moral support. I am grateful to all of them. I also thank my friends and relatives for their moral support and encouragement. Thanks are also due to my friends especially Dr. B.S. Virk, (NJSA College, Jalander) and Mr. Parvinder, Arora (STG, Chandigarh) who made my study comfortable in Punjab during my field survey.

I am highly grateful to the administrative and library staff of the XLRI Jamshedpur, IILM, New Delhi and IIPA, New Delhi for their assistance and help in collection of research material. My thanks are also due to the Librarian, Department of Commerce, University of Kashmir, for her cooperation and help in collection of research material.

I acknowledge my deepest sense of gratitude to my dear parents, to whom this work is dedicated for their affection, encouragement and blessings. I would be failing my duty if I do not express my gratitude to my in-laws for their constant encouragement and moral support.

I cannot part without acknowledging the wholehearted cooperation and steadfast devotion I received from my spouse throughout the completion of this study

Finally, I am thankful to M/S Universal Computers, Sadrabal, Srinagar for computerizing the present work so cheerfully and carefully.

Mushtaq A. Bhat

1

Introduction

This introductory chapter begins with throwing light on the importance of service sector at national and international level followed by a review of some major studies on service marketing. It also highlights that high service quality performance—the core of services marketing, produces measurable benefits in terms of profit maximization, cost savings and market share enlargement. The need for the study followed by its underlying objectives and organizational design also feature in this chapter.

The perception about services, in the past, was confined to 'work only with service motto'. Today we find that services have been commercialized and professionalised. It is due to the emergence of materialistic age in which financial health of an organisation and economic status of an individual are regarded to be important parameters to evaluate soundness, perfection and excellence. This has helped germination of the seeds of competition for which, either to maintain existence or to thrive, it is imperative to be professional so that the faculties are enriched for generating profits, maximizing wealth, multiplying capital, excelling in competition and establishing leadership. The industrial transformation, thus, opens doors for social, cultural and economic transformation, which transforms the nature and character of our needs. Today, we prefer to spend our disposable income on the multi-faceted sophisticated amenities and facilities developed by the industrial world. All these developments in the socio-economic and cultural fabrics have helped the emergence of service sector in a formal way.

International Scenario of Service Sector

The developed countries have been successful in tapping the potential of services sector by setting up new paradigm. The tremendous growth of service sector has resulted in its increased importance to the world economies (see for details Table 1.1). For instance in 1948, 54% of GDP of United States was generated by services and the increasing trend of the use of services has continued with services contributing 72% of the U.S. GDP in the year 1999. Table 1.1 clearly reveals that United States is not unique in its conversion to a service economy. Similar changes have taken place elsewhere. Today, service sector dominates the economies of other nations like Belgium, Italy, Japan, Jordan, Maxico, Norway, Singapore to name a few, as is clear from Table 1.1.

As countries develop, the role of agriculture in the economy declines and that of services rises. All developed countries have more than 50% of GDP and employment derived from services. A particular characteristic of the development of service employment over time is that it is less sensitive to business cycle fluctuations than other types of employment.

The large and rapidly growing services sector in most countries has resulted in the emergence of a new breed of larger and more sophisticated service companies. Fortune Magazine annually compiles a ranking of the world's leading service companies, separated into eight categories – diversified services, commercial banks, diversified financials, saving institutions, life insurance, retailers, transportation and utilities. These major service firms are now increasingly looking to international markets in search of future markets. Globalisation

TABLE 1.1

Gross Domestic Product and its Sectoral Share for the Year 1999

	Value added as % of GDP		
Economy	*Agriculture*	*Industry*	*Services*
Brazil	09	29	62
Belgium	01	28	71
Bulgaria	18	27	55
Colombia	14	25	61
Hungary	06	34	60
Italy	03	30	67
Japan	02	37	61
Jordan	02	27	71
Kazakhstan	10	30	60
Kenya	27	17	56
Lebanon	12	27	61
Maxico	05	27	68
Norway	02	32	66
Pakistan	26	25	49
Russia	08	34	58
Singapore	0	36	64
Turkey	18	26	56
United States	02	26	72
Uruguay	09	29	62

Source: World Development Report 2001-2002, Oxford University Press, New York, pp. 296-297.

is assisting the process of defusing new service developments across national boundaries and as the interest in globalization intensifies, service firms will make efforts to establish their international networks and brands.

Indian Scenario

The service sector in the Indian economy accounted for

29 per cent of the total GDP at current prices in 1950-51. This share increased by 32.9 per cent in 1970-71, 36 per cent in 1980-81, 42.5 per cent in 1994-95 and 54.2 in 2000-01, as is clear from following Table 1.2. It shows a sharp increase in the relative share of services sector in the decades of 1970's and 1980's. Such a positive trend is found in almost all the developing countries.

TABLE 1.2

Gross Domestic Product and its Sectoral Share

At Current Prices Year	*% Sectoral Share in GDP*		
	Agriculture	*Industry*	*Services*
1950-51	55.8	15.2	29.0
1960-61	45.8	20.7	33.5
1970-71	45.2	21.9	32.9
1980-81	38.1	25.9	36.0
1990-91	31.0	29.3	39.7
1991-92	31.3	27.8	40.9
1992-93	30.6	28.3	41.1
1993-94	33.6	23.7	42.7
1994-95	33.0	24.5	42.5
1995-96	30.8	25.6	43.6
1996-97	31.5	24.9	43.6
1997-98	30.4	24.7	44.9
1998-99	26.6	21.9	51.5
1999-2000	25.2	21.8	53.0
2000-2001	24.0	21.8	54.2

Source: 1. *Statistical Outline of India (2000-2001)*, Department of Economics and Statistics, Tata Services Ltd., Mumbai – 400001.
2. Central Statistical Organisation, Government of India.

The growth rates and sectoral composition of Gross Domestic Product at factor cost has been shown in Table 1.3.

TABLE 1.3

Growth Rates and Sectoral Composition of Real Gross Domestic Product (At 1993-94 Prices)

Sector	*Growth Rate*			*1994-95 to*	*Share in real GDP*		
	*2000-2001**	*1999-2000**	*1998-1999@*	*1999-2000*	*2000-2001#*	*1999-2000**	*1998-99@*
1. **Agriculture & Allied Activities**	**0.2**	**0.7**	**7.1**	**3.2**	**24.0**	**25.2**	**26.6**
of which:					(0.9)	(2.8)	(28.5)
Agriculture	—	0.3	7.9	3.1			
2. **Industry**	**5.3**	**6.1**	**2.8**	**7.4**	**21.8**	**21.8**	**21.9**
of which:					(22.3)	(20.8)	(9.8)
a) Mining and quarrying	3.7	1.7	1.3	4.8	2.3	2.3	2.4
b) Manufacturing	5.6	6.8	2.5	7.9	17.1	17.1	17.0
c) Electricity, gas & water supply	4.7	5.2	6.4	6.8	2.4	2.5	2.5
3. **Services**	**7.5**	**9.4**	**8.0**	**8.5**	**54.2**	**53.0**	**51.5**
of which:					(76.8)	(76.5)	(61.8)
a) Construction	5.5	8.1	6.1	6.4	5.1	5.1	5.0
b) Trade, hotels & Restaurants	$6.9	7.9	7.0	9.2	$22.3	14.6	14.4
c) Transport, Storage & Communication	—	8.3	7.3	8.7	—	7.3	7.2
d) Financing, insurance, real estate and business services	9.1	10.1	8.4	8.5	13.2	12.7	12.3
e) Community, social & personal services	7.8	11.8	9.9	8.5	13.5	13.2	12.6
4. **Gross Domestic Product at** Factor Cost	**5.2**	**6.4**	**6.6**	**6.7**	**100.0**	**100.0**	**100.0**

\# : Revised Estimates * : Quick Estimates

@ : Provisional Estimates — : Not separately available

$: Corresponds to 'trade, hotels and restaurants' and 'transport, storage and communication'.

Note: Figures in brackets indicate relative contribution of the sectors to the real GDP growth.

Source: Central Statistical Organisation, Government of India.

The table clearly reveals that the share from primary as well as secondary sector to total GDP was only 24.0 per cent and

21.8 per cent respectively during the year 2000-01 while as the contribution from services sector to GDP was the highest, i.e. 54.2 per cent during the same year which consists of 5.1 per cent of construction, 22.3 per cent of trade, hotels and restaurants, 13.2 per cent of finance, insurance, real estate and business services and 13.5 per cent of community, social and personal services.

The table also shows sectoral growth rates from 1994-95 to 1999-2000 of Gross Domestic Product. It is evident from the data that the growth rate of services during 1994-95 to 1999-2000 is highest (8.5) while as growth rates of industry followed by agriculture during the same year (7.4 and 3.2 respectively) are lowest. The overall GDP growth rates decreased significantly from 6.4 per cent in 1999-2000 to 5.2 per cent in 2000-01. In particular, the growth rate of construction sector reduced considerably to 5.5 per cent during 2000-01 over that of the previous year. Financing, insurance, real estate and business services also performed poorly with a growth rate of 9.1 per cent only in 2000-01 compared to a growth rate of 10.1 per cent in 1999-2000. The unsatisfactory performance of the financial and real estate sectors was due to a negative growth rate in banking and insurance, as a result of the decline in the output of non-banking financial institutions (*Economic Survey 2001-02*, p. 5). Community, social and personal services also grew at a much lower rate in 2000-01 as compared with that of the previous year. The Tables (1.1-1.3) show a steady growth of services sector in Indian economy as is also clear from its contribution to GDP. The difference in GDP figures shows distinctively the growing importance of services sector in Indian economy.

Services: A Conceptual Construct

To develop clarity on services as a concept, it is desirable to look at the way various researches have defined it over the last three decades. One of the first to define services was the American Marketing Association, which, as early as in 1960 defined services as, "activities, benefits, or satisfactions, which are offered for sale, or provided in connection with the sale of goods" (Shanker, 1999). This definition took a limited view of services as it tied the services with goods. The individual identity of the services has not been recognized. The services may have their individual entity and they may not necessarily be tied to the sale of a physical product. Regan (1963) suggested that, "services represent either intangibles yielding satisfactions directly (transportation, housing), or intangibles yielding satisfactions jointly when purchased either with commodities or other services (credit delivery)". For the first time services were considered as pure intangibles, capable of providing satisfaction to the customer and marketable like tangible products. Robert (1964) considered service as, "a market transaction by an enterprise or entrepreneur where the object of market transaction is other than the transfer of ownership of a tangible commodity". He recognized three broad areas of services as (a) the right to possess and use a product (rented goods services), (b) the custom creation, repair, or improvement of a product (owned goods services), and (c) no product elements but rather an experience or what might be termed as experiential possession (non-goods services). Bessom (1973) proposed that "for the consumer, services are activities offered for sale that provides valuable benefits or satisfactions, activities that he cannot perform for himself or that he chooses not to perform for himself". Blois (1974) defined service as, an activity offered for sale which yields benefits and satisfactions without leading to a physical change in the form of a good". Stanton (1994), the noted marketing scholar, thought of services as, "separately identifiable, intangible activities which provide want satisfaction when marketed to consumers and/or industrial users and which are not necessarily tied to the sale of a product or other service".

All the above mentioned concepts have one common limitation i.e. they do not recognize that services need to be looked beyond the product to which it is attached or the person who provides it. A service attached to a customer for a product he owns is called customer service, and a service to the same customer by a doctor is a health service. A service by human beings is known by its deeds. Thus, services are deeds, acts or performances (Berry, 1980). The complexity to this simple definition is added when we realize that there are neither pure services nor pure tangible products. Nevertheless, the definition given by Kotler and Bloom (1984) does reach the fineness. They consider service as, "any activity or benefit that one party can offer to another that is essentially intangible and does not result in the ownership of anything. Its production may or may not be tied to a physical product".

Gummesson (1987), while highlighting the intangible nature of services, defined services as, "something which can be bought but which you cannot drop on your foot". This definition also pointed out one basic characteristic that the services can be exchanged even though they are not tangible. However, Gronroos (1990) proposed a working definition of services, as according to him, "a service is an activity or series of activities of more or less intangible nature that normally, not necessarily, take place in interactions between the customer and service employees and /or physical resources or goods and/or systems of the service provider, which are provided as solution to the customer problems". Philip Kottler (1999) gives comparatively a more comprehensive and refined concept. According to him, "service is an act or performance that one party can offer to another that is essentially intangible and does not result in the ownership of anything. Its production may or may not be tied to a physical product".

On a review of different definitions on services, it can safely be concluded that any definition on services is inherently restrictive because of unique service characteristics. However, there is almost unanimity among the researchers that services are intangible activities, benefits or satisfactions that are offered for sale and does not result in the ownership of anything.

Relying on this simple definition of services, it becomes clear that services are produced not only by service businesses but are also integral to the offerings of many manufactured goods producers. For example, car manufacturers offer warranties and repair services for their cars, computer manufacturers offer warranties, industrial equipment producers offer delivery and maintenance services and also photocopier producers offer after sale services. All of these services are examples of activities, benefits, satisfactions, deeds and performances. The variety of definitions highlighted above explains confusion or disagreements people have while discussing services or describing industries that comprise the services sector of the economy. The above examples also make it clear that it is nearly impossible to find a pure tangible good without services attached, particularly in the age of 'maxi marketing'.

Goods Versus Services Marketing

There is a general agreement that inherent differences between goods and services exist and that they result in unique, or at least different, management challenges for service businesses and for manufacturers that offer services as a core offering (Zeithaml, et. al., 1985). These differences and associated marketing implications are given as under:

Comparison of Goods and Services and Associated Marketing Implications

Goods	*Services*	*Resulting Implications*
Tangible	Intangible	Services cannot be inventoried. Services cannot be patented. Services cannot be readily displayed or communicated. Pricing is difficult.
Standardised	Heterogeneous	Service delivery and customer satisfaction depend on employee actions. Service quality depends on many uncontrollable factors. There is no sure knowledge that the service delivered matches what was planned and promoted.
Production separate from consumption	Simultaneous production and consumption	Customers participate in and affect the transaction. Customers affect each other. Employees affect the service outcome. Decentralization may be essential. Mass production is difficult.
Non-perishable	Perishable	It is difficult to synchronize supply and demand with services. Services cannot be returned or resold.

Source: Parasuraman A., Valaric A. Zaithaml, and Berry Leonard L., (1985) "A Conceptual Model of Service Quality and Its Implications for Future Research" Journal of Marketing, Vol. 49, Fall, pp. 41-50.

Intangibility

The most basic and universally cited (e.g., Bateson, 1977; Berry, 1980; Lovelock, 1981), difference between goods and services is intangibility. Because services are performances or actions rather than objects, they cannot be seen, felt, tasted, or touched in the same manner as we can sense tangible goods. Intangibility, according to Bateson (1979), is the critical goods service distinction from which all other differences emerge.

Simultaneous Production and Consumption

Whereas goods are produced first, then sold and consumed, most services are sold first and then produced and consumed simultaneously (Regan, 1963). A passenger on an airplane first purchases a ticket and then flies, consuming the in-flight service as it is produced. Thus the consumer becomes involved in the production process (Carmen and Langeard, 1980). The simultaneity of production and consumption poses two special considerations for services marketing. First, since the individuals providing the services (nurses, bank tellers, barbers, repair specialists) come directly in contact with the customer, they must recognize their marketing role as well as their production role. Second, because many services require personal contact between the seller and the buyer, service firms must pay special attention to location (Gronroos, 1978).

Heterogeneity

Because services are performances, frequently produced by humans, no two services are precisely alike. The employees delivering the service frequently are the service in the customer's eyes, and people may differ in their performance from day to day or even hour to hour. Heterogeneity also results because no two customers are precisely alike; each will have unique demands or experience the service in a unique way. Thus, the heterogeneity connected with services is largely the result of human interaction (between and among employees and customers) and all of the vagaries that accompany it (Booms and Bitner 1981; Langeard et.al. 1981).

Perishability

Perishability refers to the fact that services cannot be saved, stored, resold, or returned because they are performances. A seat on an airplane or in a restaurant, an hour of a lawyers time, a medical/academic advice or telephone line capacity cannot be reclaimed and used or resold at a later time which is quite in contrast to goods (Zeithaml, et al., 1985).

The above review of literature suggests that each unique characteristic of service leads to specific problems for service marketers and necessitates special strategies for dealing with them (for details see Zeithaml, et.al., 1985).

Interest in the problems of marketing of service organisations is growing rapidly. This may be explained in part by rising levels of competition in many parts of the service sector. Service marketing emerged late because of perceived lack of need for it in times when demand exceeded supply and competitive pressures were few. Now competition is increasing and consumers are demanding more and better services. Growing sophistication among consumers means that service standards are changing steadily.

Most of the developed countries have been successful in tapping the potential of the services sector as is evident from the growing contribution of services sector to their GDPs. These countries have realised and comprehended properly the peculiar characteristics of services and achieved perfection in service quality. The services in these countries are marketed just like physical products. But all this is yet to be achieved in India where the competition is non-existent in majority of the service sector organisations. Moreover, in majority of the cases service organisations still enjoy a sellers market, causing excessive demand than supply. This gap in demand and supply has reduced quality of service.

In India, some of the service areas, where marketing of service has been thrown open to competition, the results are very encouraging and the quality of service has improved a lot. For example, the incoming of the satellite channels has forced the traditional Doordarshan to improve the quality of service, which it has done tremendously. The Prasar Bharti Bill, which has been passed to make Doordarshan an independent corporation on the pattern of B.B.C., has immensely changed the programmes of Doordarshan and brought it in competition with other channels. Similarly, airlines, telecom, mobile phones/cellular phones and Internet Service Providers (ISP) companies are fighting a do or die battle in the field of quality of service. Due to this competition in the services sector, some of the service business houses are bound to vanish if quality service is not preached as the core philosophy of business.

Thus, it is evident that the quality of anything, whether it is a physical product or intangible one, depends upon the level of competition. As it will grow, the quality will also grow and in the absence of the competition, the product or the service takes the shape of monopoly and the managers hardly think of improving it. In the absence of competition quality becomes the last priority. Another factor that is responsible for lesser share of services in GDP in India is its unaccountability in earlier times. The services in majority of the cases were in the unorganised sector and hence remained unaccounted for. Moreover, in some of the cases, they were rendered free of cost. In these days of specilisation, firstly the services have been accounted for and secondly they are being charged. If the service is free, its quality is hardly cared for. Paid services and tough competition, in a chosen service market, forces service providers to improve quality standards.

Need for the Present Study

Interest in service quality is obvious when one thinks about it. Poor quality places a firm at a competitive disadvantage. If customers perceive quality as unsatisfactory; they may be quick to take their business elsewhere. Recent years have witnessed a veritable explosion of discontent with service quality at a time when the quality of many manufactured goods seems to have improved significantly.

From a marketing standpoint, a key issue is whether customers notice differences in quality between competing suppliers or not! Improving quality in the eyes of customers pays off for the companies that provide it. Data from the Profit Impact of Market Strategy (PIMS) research show that a perceived quality advantage leads to higher profits (Buzzell and Gale, 1987). Berry and Parasuraman (1991) also hold the view that high quality service gives credibility to the field sales force and advertising, stimulates favorable word-of-mouth communications, enhances customers' perception of value, and boosts the morale and loyalty of employees and customers alike. Thus, it is clear that service quality offers a way of achieving success among competing services. Particularly where a number of firms that offer nearly identical services are competing within a small area, such as banks, establishing service quality may be the only way of differentiating oneself. Such differentiation can yield a higher proportion of consumers' choices and, hence, mean the difference between financial success and failure. In a liberalized and competitive environment, therefore, only those banks would be effective in delivering goods, which provide excellent service quality. Almost, all the banks perform same functions. Therefore, the customer takes into account the relative efficiency while choosing a particular bank. Moreover, banks carry on business with public money and, therefore, customers expect better service from them.

The most recent trend in many service organisations is to consider quality service as a critical factor in enabling them to achieve a differential advantage over their competitors (Albrecht and Zemke, 1985; Berry, Bennett and Brown, 1989; Leonard and Sasser, 1982; Ross and Shetty, 1985). Increasingly, quality is becoming a key variable in strategic planning. Further, the organisations which are becoming leaders in quality service are characterized by the commitment of top management and a corporate culture that encourages a consumer and quality focus throughout the company (Albrecht and Zemke, 1985; Marshall, 1985). In India, may academicians and practitioners (Brahmanandam and Narayana, 1990; Elias, 1982; Nageswar and Pramod, 1990; Nageswar, 1987; Nandakumar, 1995; Sesha Sai, 1999; and Sundaram, 1984) have highlighted the need for better service quality in banks, mostly public sector banks, and offered guidelines for improvement in bank services. These studies have also warned public sector banks that if the present trend of customer dissatisfaction continues unabated, time is not far away when these banks will loose their valuable customers to competitors (especially private and foreign).

In the light of above research findings quality service is critical to banks success particularly in today's increasingly competitive environment. In spite of the tremendous importance of service quality in banks, the subject has remained almost academically unexplored in India. No comprehensive study has, so for, been conducted to study service quality and its dimensions in banks. The present study is aimed at filling up this gap in existing literature.

Objectives of the Study

The study has been conducted with the following precise objectives in view:

1. To study service quality and its dimensions in banks through SERVQUAL Scale.
2. To examine the expectations and perceptions of bank customers and bank officials regarding service quality in banks under study.
3. To make a comparison across private and public sector banks as also national and foreign banks operating in India on critical service quality dimensions.
4. To suggest, on the basis of study results, ways and means for improving service quality in banks

with a view to make overall banking service more effective and efficient.

Organization of the Study

The subject matter of the study has been divided in seven broad chapters. The first chapter of the study, besides highlighting the contribution of service sector in GDP at national and international level, reviews the concept and peculiar characteristics of services. It also highlights the need for the present study. In chapter second, a critical review of literature on the subject has been made with a view to emphasize important contributions on the subject and the areas of deficiency. At the end, the chapter brings to light agenda for future research. Chapter third discusses research methodology, area of study, sample size, demographic makeup of respondents, besides the tools of analysis. Chapter fourth is devoted to empirical findings regarding quality of service and its dimensions in banks. Chapter fifth presents empirical findings related to expectations and perceptions of customers. It also makes a comparison of perceptions of bank officials and respective customers regarding quality of service in banks. In chapter sixth empirical findings regarding service quality variations in banks have been discussed. It also presents a comparison across private and public sector banks as also national and foreign banks operating in India, regarding various service quality dimensions. The last chapter is devoted to integrate research findings and offers suggestions for improving service quality in banks with a view to make over all banking service more effective and efficient.

2

Review of Literature

A general tenet in marketing and business holds that high quality goods and services are favored in the market place. As a result of this widespread belief in the tenet, service organizations have placed service quality at the top of a list of strategic constructs. The present chapter, besides throwing light briefly on marketing developments in banking services in India, covers a review of literature on service quality, customer service, and banking technology. The existing literature on the subject has been critically evaluated with a view to place in proper perspective the important contributions in the field, identify deficiencies and provide a framework for future studies in the area of service quality.

Bank Marketing in India

Marketing came into banks in the late 1950s, not in the form of marketing concept, but in the form of advertising and promotion (Kotlar, 1980; Ramachandra, 1992; Scredhar, 1991). In India, however, the importance of marketing was realized much later. During 1950s, Indian banks were more conservative and inward looking, concerned mainly with their profits. As a matter of fact, competition was not in existence. On the one side of the fence was State Bank of India alone, enjoying Government patronage and on the other side were private commercial banks, local by orientation, primarily serving the interests of the controlling business houses. It was the phase of select banking and even the communication through the media was looked down upon with contempt as something against the tenets of banking culture. Even the advertisements released till 1966 were very few and far between (Saxena, 1985).

However, after nationalization of fourteen major commercial banks in 1969, banks woke up from their splendid isolation and found themselves in a highly competitive and rapidly changing environment, with competition becoming fierce day by day. Banks approach towards customers and market underwent a change and focus was gradually shifted to marketing their products. The first major step in this direction of marketing was initiated by State Bank of India when in 1972 it reorganized itself on the basis of major market segments – small industries and small businesses, agriculture, commercial and institutional, and personal and service banking (Rajan, 1992). Again in 1973, the State Bank of India took yet another major leap forward in the direction of marketing when it took upon itself the responsibility of involving itself in the neighborhood affairs and winning the cooperation of community development efforts (Saxena, 1988). Realizing the duty towards community development, individual banks, in order to have close contact with the masses, also started actively participating in many of the social, economic and education functions/ceremonies arranged by different organizations (Aul, 1994). In the early 1980s, banks started thinking in terms of product development, market penetration and market development (Ajit, 1986; Bhattacharya and Ghose, 1989; Rayndu, 1990). Banks also accelerated their process of equipping their staff with the marketing capabilities and attitudes through different programmes.

During the last two decades, marketing development in banks has undergone revolutionary changes. Apart from unprecedented growth and functional diversification, there has, in fact, been a change in the concept, precept and outlook of banking (Ghose, 1987). The post-nationalization era witnessed a complete transformation of Indian banking from 'class' banking to 'mass' banking, from 'asset based' lending to 'production oriented' lending and from 'elite' banking to 'social banking'. This present phase of market-oriented banking or bank marketing started in early eighties. The new trend of disinter-mediation and high degree of competition contributed to the development of this kind of banking.

The above discussion leads us to conclude that adoption of marketing concept in Indian banking as a conscious and organized effort is of recent origin. Marketing has emerged now as the core business philosophy for financial service companies and successes belongs to ones who excel in customer mindedness and responsiveness. In a liberalized and competitive environment, therefore, only those banks would be successful which provide excellent service quality. This is because the prime function of banks is the creation and delivery of customer needed service in a customer-satisfying manner (Sundaram, 1984). Delivering higher levels of service quality is the strategy that is increasingly being offered as a key to service provider's efforts to position themselves more effectively in the marketplace (Brown and Swartz, 1989; Parasuraman, et al., 1988). Almost all banks perform same functions. Therefore, customer takes into account the relative efficiency while choosing a particular bank. Moreover, banks carry on business with public money and, therefore, customers expect better service from them. Customers, employees and changing business environment drive the need for customer service/service quality.

Customers, be they individuals, households, or organizations, are increasingly aware of alternatives on offer, in relation to services and provider organizations, and also of rising standards of service. Consequently, expectations rise (Gronroos, 1984; Leonard and Sasser, 1982; Takeuchi and Quelch, 1983) and consumers became more critical of the quality of service received (Susan and Dong, 1994), and so companies can never be complacent. In addition, knowledge of the costs and benefits of keeping customers, relative to attracting new ones (Buzzell and Wiersema, 1981; Schoeffler, Buzzell and Heany, 1974; Takeuchi and Quelch, 1983 and more recently Barnes, 1997), draws companies attention to looking after present customers, responding to their needs and problems, and developing long-term relationships. The costs of poor quality relate to lack of responsiveness to the customer, dissatisfied customers, complaints and adverse word-of-mouth communication, and dissatisfied employees (Crosby, 1979; Goodman, Marra and Brigham 1986).

Looking after ***employees*** is also an opportunity for an organisation. As companies become large, they may also become anonymous and bureaucratic (Sundaram, 1984). Communication may deteriorate and relationships (between customers and customer contact personnel, between customer contact staff and back-room staff, and between staff and management) may suffer (Benjamin and Bowen, 1993; Benjamin, 1980; Bitner, Booms and Tetreault, 1990). However, companies are realizing that commitment to employees brings rewards.

The ***business environment*** is characterized by economic, legal and technological changes. For example, in financial services, the law resulting in deregulation has increased competition between financial service providers and brought retailers into the industry, thus providing more choice for the consumer. In a competitive environment, therefore, companies can react by emphasizing operations and financial efficiency and/or more focussed product and market strategies (Kotler, 1999). Superior customer service may, therefore, be seen as a mechanism to achieve differentiation and a competitive advantage, and so become integral to the overall direction and strategy of an organisation (Brown and Swartz, 1989; Panasuraman, et al., 1988).

During the last one decade, a number of marketing scholars and practitioners have placed considerable importance on the management of quality. Indeed several authors (e.g., Barnes, 1997; Garvin, 1983; Schoeffler, et al., 1974; Takeuchi and Quelch, 1983; Buzzell and Wiersema, 1981; Leonard and Sasser, 1982) support that tenet (quality) and further suggest that high service quality performance produces measurable benefits in profit, cost savings, and market share. As a result of this evidence and a widespread belief in the tenet companies have placed service quality at the top of a list of strategic construct important in the next several years (Uttal, 1987).

In light of above research findings and as a background for the present study, some major studies on service quality, customer service, and banking technology are reviewed in this chapter.

Service Quality

Despite the appreciation of the importance of service quality in strategic planning and for corporate success, there are no clear cut-definitions of quality or dimensions for setting quality standards and measuring subsequent quality delivered and received. Most of the suggested definitions focus on meeting customer needs and requirements. For example, service quality is "a measure of how well the service delivered matches customer's expectations" (Lewis and Booms, 1983), or "providing the customer with what he wants, when he wants it, and at acceptable cost, within the operating constraints of the business", and "providing a better service than the customer expects" (Lewis, 1988). Too often the term 'quality' is used as it were a variable itself such as conformance to specifications, the degree to which customer specifications are satisfied, a fair exchange of price and value, fitness for use, freedom from variation and doing it right the first time (Garvin, 1988; Kotlar, 1999; Woodruffe, 1998).

Additionally, a number of definitions refer to the importance of the client's/ customer's perceptions of quality (Takeuchi and Quelch, 1983) which are consumer's attitudes or judgements resulting from comparisons by consumers of expectations of service with their perceptions of actual service performance (Berry, et al., 1985,1988; Gronroos, 1982; Lewis and Boom, 1983). Berry (1980), along with Booms and Bitner (1981), argue that, due to intangible nature of services, customer use elements associated with the physical environment when evaluating service quality. Managing the evidence and using the environmental psychology are often seen as important marketing tools. Levitt (1981) proposes that customers use appearances to make judgements about realities, and less tangible a product the more powerful is the effect of packaging in judging that product. Hostage (1975) for his part, believes that a service firm's contact personnel comprise the major determinant of service quality, while Lewis and Booms (1983) propose that service quality resides in the ability of the service firm to satisfy its customer needs, i.e. customer satisfaction, Purasuraman, et al., (1985) found that consumer's perceptions of quality are influenced by various gaps which lead to service quality shortfalls and, in particular, that the "quality perceived in a service is a function of the gap between customer's desires/expectations and their perceptions of the service that is actually received," i.e., service quality is a measure of how well the service delivered meets the expectations of service. Quality has, thus, become one of the main concerns of company officials (Leonard and Sasser, 1982) and is becoming a strategic variable which greatly affects marketing and production policies in many service firms.

While the substance and determinants of quality may be

undefined, its importance to firms and consumers is unequivocal. There is enough evidence that demonstrates the strategic benefits of quality in contributing to market share and returns on investment (Adrian, 1995; Anderson and Zeithaml, 1984; Bateson, 1995; Berry and Parasuraman, 1991; Buzzell and Wiersema, 1981; Devlin and Dong, 1996; Reichheld and Sasser, 1990), lowering manufacturing cost and improving productivity (Garvin, 1983; Kotlar, 1999; Leonard and Sasser, 1982). Devlin and Dong (1996) believe that improved service quality also cuts costs because companies have fewer customers to replace, less corrective work to do, fewer inquires and complaints to handle, and less employee turnover and dissatisfaction with which to deal.

Assessing quality is more complex for services than it is for manufactured products because services are intangible and cannot always be measured or tested before delivery, and each service delivery is unique compared to the previous one. Further, services are produced and consumed simultaneously, with the customer actively participating.

Efforts in defining and measuring quality have come largely from the goods sector. Knowledge about goods quality, however, is insufficient to understand service quality. Three well documented characteristics of service – intangibility, heterogeneity, and inseparability – must be acknowledged for a full understanding of service quality.

> ***Intangibility:*** The first and fundamental characteristic of service universally accepted, is intangibility (Bateson, 1977; Berry, 1980; Gronroos, 1978; Gronroos, 1979; Lovelock, 1981; Woodruffe, 1998). Because services are performances, rather than objects, they cannot be seen, felt, tasted or touched in the same manner in which goods can be sensed. Most services cannot be counted,

measured, inventoried, tasted and verified in advance of sale to assure quality. Because of intangibility, the firm may find it difficult to understand how consumers perceive their services and evaluate service quality (Zeithaml and Bitner, 1996).

Heterogeneity: Heterogeneity concerns the potential for high variability in the performance of services. The quality is the essence of service and can vary from producer to producer, from customer to customer, and from day to day. Heterogeneity in service output is a particular problem for labour intensive services. Consistency of behavior from service personnel is difficult to assure because what the firm intends to deliver may be entirely different from what the consumers perceive (Bateson, 1995; Booms and Bitner, 1981; Carman and Langeard, 1980; Parasuraman, et al., 1985).

Inseparability: Third, production and consumption of many services are inseparable (Berry, 1980; Carman and Langeard, 1980; Gronroos, 1978; and Zeithaml and Bitner, 1996). Whereas goods are first produced, then sold and then consumed, services are first sold, then produced and consumed simultaneously. In labour intensive services, for example, quality occurs during service delivery, usually in an interaction between the client and the contact person from the service firm. The service firm also has less managerial control over quality in services where consumer participation is intense, as client affects the process. Under such circumstances, the consumers' feedback becomes critical to the quality of service performance.

Due to their intangibility, heterogeneity, perishable nature and the inseparability of production and consumption, service quality becomes difficult to conceptualize and measure. Therefore, when marketing intangibles, the major concern of business managers becomes the provision and control of symbols and tangible clues used by the customer in evaluating the service. Quality is thus relative and subjective, and depends on the perceptions and expectations that the customer has with respect to service offering. On a review of literature on the subject (service quality characteristics) the following three themes emerge:

1. *Service Quality is More Difficult to Evaluate*

Service quality is more difficult for consumers to evaluate than goods quality. Therefore, the criteria that customers use to evaluate service quality may be more difficult for marketers to comprehend. Unlike goods, when purchasing services, fever tangible cues exist. In most cases, tangible evidence is limited to service provider's physical facilities, equipment and personnel. Customer's assessment of the quality of health care, education and training, insurance and banking etc. services are more complex than their assessment of quality of automobiles or other tangible products. Because of service intangibility, a firm may find it more difficult to understand how consumers perceive services and service quality. When a service provider knows how the service will be evaluated by the consumer, he will be able to suggest how to influence these evaluations in a desired direction (Gronroos, 1982).

2. *Quality is a Comparison Between Expectations and Performance*

Service quality perceptions result from a comparison of consumer expectations with actual service performance. Lewis and Booms (1983) suggests that service quality involves comparing customer expectations to the performances obtained from the service provided. Quality is thus perceived as the manner in which services, through their delivery system, satisfy customer needs. Delivering quality service means conforming to customer expectations on a consistent basis. Gronroos (1982) contends that consumers compare the service they expect with perceptions of the service they receive in evaluating service quality. To earn good reputation in quality, the firm must match or exceed customer expectations.

3. *Quality Evaluations Involve Outcomes and Processes*

Customers do not evaluate service quality solely on the outcome of service. They also involve evaluation of the process of service delivery. Gronroos (1984) establishes a distinction between two forms of service quality:

(a) Technical quality – which involves what the customer is actually receiving from the service,

(b) Functional quality – which involves the manner in which the service in delivered to include the attitudes and behavior, appearance and personality, service mindedness, accessibility and approachability of customer contact personnel – together with the corporate image dimension of quality. Functional quality in seen as being predominant in the customers' evaluative process. Lehtinan and Lehtinan (1984) proposes three major determinants of service quality: (i) institutional quality, i.e. corporate image; (ii) physical quality, which corresponds to the physical environment associated with the service – producing system; and (iii) interactive quality, which involves the interactions between contact personnel and customers as well as interaction among the customers themselves.

Dimensions of Service Quality

As the understanding of service quality has emerged, researchers have developed conceptualizations of the dimensions of service quality. Barry (1980), along with Booms and Bitner (1981), argue that due to intangible nature of services, customers use elements associated with physical environment when evaluating service quality. Levitt (1981) proposes that customers use appearances to make judgements about realities, and the less tangible a product the more powerful is the effect of packaging in judging the product. Gummesson and Gronroos (1987) synthesized the Gronrooss' Model with one from manufacturing and incorporate design, production, delivery and relational dimensions of quality. Hostage (1975) believes that a service firm's contact personnel comprise the major determinant of service quality.

Carson and Gilmore (1989) believe that essentially customers have both instrumental and psychological expectations about a product or service performance, where expectations relate to quantifiable, hard data and qualitative soft data. Hard data are described by smith (1987) as relating to performance and reliability standards or any tangible dimensions. Soft data are those concerned with descriptions of and knowledge of customers' feelings, perceptions and requirements. Consequently these aspects of service performance are more difficult to measure and more suited to the use of 'Soft' qualitative data (Carson and Gilmore, 1989).

Gronroos (1984) stressed the need for managers to create good functional quality in order to satisfy customers. Carson and Gilmore (1989) warn against the tendency to concentrate on more tangible aspect of service delivery just because they are easier to measure and highlight the neglect of the intangible aspects. They argue that in order to successfully implement a market- led quality improvement initiative, an integrated approach focusing on the quality of both the tangible and intangible aspects of all marketing offerings is required.

Parasuraman, et al., (1985), Parasuraman et al., (1988) offer the most widely reported set of service quality dimensions: tangibility, reliability, responsiveness, communications, credibility, security, competence, courtesy, understanding/knowing the customer, and access. Subsequent factor analysis and testing by Parasuraman, et al.al., (1988) condensed these into five categories – tangibility, reliability, responsiveness, assurance, and empathy- to which Gronroos (1988) added a sixth dimension – recovery. Their ongoing research has produced a well received conceptual framework known as the Gaps Model and a measurement instrument, referred to as SERVQUAL, for assessing service quality. While there is a healthy and for most part productive debate regarding the dimensionality of SERVQUAL across industries, and the precise wording of the SERVQUAL items, researchers generally agree that the scale items are good predictors of overall service quality (Babakus and Boller, 1992; Bolton and Drew, 1991a; Bolton and Drew, 1991b; Brown and Swartz, 1989; Carman, 1990; Cronin and Taylor, 1992; Parasuraman, et al., (1991). The debate underscores the importance of the topic and the significance of the contribution to data. Such interchange will help refine the meaning of service quality.

Measurement of Service Quality

The current measurement of perceived service quality can be traced to the research of Parasuraman, Zeithaml, and Berry. These authors originally identified ten determinants of services quality based on a series of focus group sessions (1985).

They subsequently developed SERVQUAL (1988), which recasts the ten determinants into five specific components. Tangibility, reliability, responsiveness, assurance and empathy (figure 1).

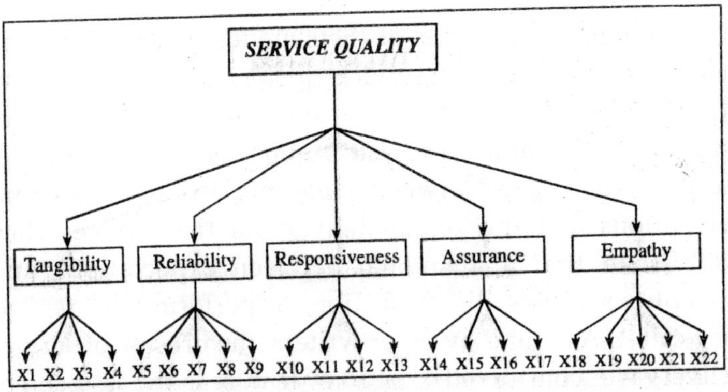

Figure 1: Dimensions of Service Quality (SERVQUAL MODEL) developed by Parasuraman et al., (1988).

The basis for identifying these five components was a factor analysis of the 22 item scale developed from focus groups and from the specific industry applications undertaken by the authors (see Parasuraman, et al. 1985, 1988; and Zeithaml, et al. 1990, for a comprehensive review). Though the veracity of conceptualizing the SERVQUAL scale as consisting of five distinct components identified by Parasuraman, et al., (1988) has been questioned (Carman, 1990), the validity of the 22 individual performance scale items that make up the SERVQUAL scale appears to be well supported both by the procedures used to develop the items and by their subsequent use as reported in the literature (Levis, 1987; Brown and Swartz, 1989; Young et al., 1994; Saleh and Ryan, 1991).

The roots of service quality research lie in early conceptual work from Carson and Gilmore (1989), Gronroos (1983), Lehtinan and Lehtinan (1982). The catalyst for much of the programme research work in the management domain of services is the conceptual model of 'SERVQUAL' presented by Parasuraman, et al., (1985) and Parasuraman, et al., (1988).

The foundation and focus of their model lay in identifying the key components of service quality, namely customer expectations and perceptions and the service delivery associated with these. The basic premise of the model is that there exists a gap between customer expectations and perceptions and the actual delivery of the service. They established that a mismatch between expectations and perceptions causes dissatisfaction, a 'performance gap' as they call it. As found by other writers, the process of service delivery was considered to be a key feature in the assessment of quality (Cronin and Taylor, 1992; Liljander and Strandrik, 1994).

Gronroos (1984) and Gilmore and Carson (1993) also identified the possible occurrence of performance gaps and in each case they attribute the gap to a failure by marketing managers to balance the marketing mix in order that customers are not led to expect more than the organisation can offer.

Limitations with SERVQUAL are highlighted by the authors themselves (Parasuraman et al., 1991) and in other research studies (Babakhus and Boller, 1992; Carman, 1990; Lewis and Mitchell, 1990; Lewis, 1993; and Smith, 1992). They relate to respondent's difficulties with negatively worded statements; using two lists of statements for the same items, the number of dimensions of service being assessed; ease of consumer assessment and timing of measurement – before, during or after a service encounter.

The conceptual model for service quality is presented as a result of an extensive exploratory investigation of quality in four service businesses. It is build upon the argument that quality is a comparison between expectations and performance and quality evaluations involve outcomes and processes. This study led to the identification of four gaps on the service providers' side that may affect service quality as perceived by the customer (with the fifth gap defined as resulting difference between perceived and expected service).

Customer Service

As business in general and the services sector in particular becomes more competitive, the need for meaningful competitive differentiation is sharpened. Increasingly this differentiation includes a search for superior performance not only on the core product but also on each of the supplementary service elements. Achieving such differentiation requires formalizing and integrating customer service activities into a professionally managed function. But unfortunately, customer service, mostly in public sector banks, has been reported by many authors and practitioners as very poor (Brahamanandam and Narayana, 1990; Elias, 1982; Nageswar, 1987; Nandakumar, 1995; Nargeswar and Pramod, 1990; Sesha Sai, 1999; and Sundaram, 1984). In fact, customer dissatisfaction in banks was realized by Government of India much earlier when it appointed the working group on customer service in banks under the leadership of Mr. R.K. Talwar in April 1975 with a view to give unified directions to banks for improvement in customer service (Bapat, 1980). The report listed following factors for customer dissatisfaction: (i) delay and inaccuracy in putting through transactions; (ii) delay and inadequacies in correspondence; (iii) delay, faulty and un-helpful decision- making; (iv) absence of elementary discipline; (v) under emphasis of staff on observance of rules and procedures; (vi) inconveniences associated with credit applications; (vii) lack of uniformity in bank charges; (viii) customer being viewed as 'faceless' unit; and (ix) general attitude of unconcern and apathy for client.

As dissatisfaction among the customers persisted, the RBI appointed a committee in September, 1990 with Shri M.N. Goiporia as its chairman to look into customer service aspects in banking. Some 80 of the Committee's 97 recommendations have since been operationalised by banks and are being followed up and reviewed (Sesha Sai, 1999). Again in 1995 a survey was conducted in Orrisa which observed that customer dissatisfaction with regard to services provided by banks are either moderate or low (Sesha Sai, 1999).

Academicians and pactioners also studied customer service in banks with a sole aim to find out areas of deficiencies and to offer guidelines to improve customer satisfaction. Ghose (1982), Goyal (1983), Ram Mohan (1983) and Rao (1984) highlighted in their studies that periodical meetings with the staff must be made compulsory in all banks so that employees do not have to resort to agitation as the only method of reprisal of their grievances, which will at the same time help in increasing customer service. Shah (1982), while studying customer service in banks, stressed the need for training of staff in areas like prompt cash payments and receipts at the counter, efficient pass book and statements service, prompt collection and remittance services, early decisions on credit applications and patient attention to complaints as he finds them major sources of customer dissatisfaction.

Bhattacharya (1989), Muniraj (1994), Nageswar and Pramad (1990) and Ramachadra (1992) in their studies highlighted branch expansion particularly in rural areas as one of the contributing factors in increasing customer dissatisfaction and concluded that to improve customer services, new innovative financial instruments have to be devised for rural banking. Lot of dissimilarities exists between a rural and urban area. Each of them is for from being homogenous. The income trends and financial assets vary considerably and therefore, rural banking deserves different banking approach. With a view to improve customer satisfaction/services Bhattacharya (1989), Nageswar and

Pramod (1990) and Muniraj (1994) stressed on market oriented banking which the authors mean a new culture, a disciplined, dedicated, professional and committed manpower, specialized bank employees, provision of quick redressal measures, extending personalized service, streamlining the age old systems and procedures.

Chidambaram (1996) in his study suggested Total Quality Management (TQM) as a means to improve customer service in banks. The author suggested twelve principles of TQM, which are aimed at customer care, quality, continuous improvement, involvement of all personnel, empowered employees, increased revenue, and reduced non-interest expenses. He firmly believes that the application of TQM will make bank lending more purposeful and will help in reducing customer grievances to a great extent. Bansal (1994) observed that banks have to design their working to create client confidence for better services. Within the given framework of rules and regulations, the operating system has to be made simple and convenient for valuable customer. For valuable customer, the author suggests, flying squads to be appointed at district headquarters, which at random should storm in different branches to have stock of state of consumer service directly from consumers. Bansal (1994) also suggested customer meetings at regular intervals, to enable them to convey their feedback and valuable suggestions.

Chaudhuri (1981) believes that customer service, by its very nature, is a dynamic concept. What is good customer service today may be regarded as poor tomorrow. Chudhuri holds the view that good customer service centers around two important aspects, viz., (i) designing of a service, and (ii) delivery of service. Both the aspects, the designing and delivery, are equally important, because bad delivery of a perfectly designed service is as harmful as perfect delivery of badly designed service, if banks want to match their services with their customers. Sundaram (1984) reports that poor services in banks are due to abnormal delays in receiving/ making payments and customers have to linger indefinitely without anybody attending on them properly at the counter while highlighting cumbersome procedures in banks. Sundaram points out that a single transaction like issuing a draft involves 15 operations, 5 checking points and 8 movements. The issue of a chequebook takes twenty to thirty minutes because the officer/accountant is always busy with cheques, vouchers and registers. Updating of the passbook also takes a long time, as the counter staff is busy with hundreds of small routine tasks.

Gurdeep (1994), observed three areas which merit special attention for the bankers as: (i) quick receiving and payment of cash; (ii) remittance of funds, whether by means of drafts, mail transfers or telegraphic transfers, with a minimum of delay; and (iii) collection of cheques, bills, dividend warrants, etc., at maximum speed. In all the three areas, he believes that banks have a lot of say, and by cutting the delay at each stage, the customer satisfaction can be improved significantly. Chidambaram (1996) believes that while dealing with a customer, banks must adopt 'CARE' approach, i.e., show courtesy, ensure accuracy, be responsible, and execute the task efficiently in order to reduce growing customer grievances. Sesha Sai (1999) believes that to overcome growing customer dissatisfaction banks should adopt two-fold strategy. First, creation of wide range of services, suitable and beneficial to the customers and second, prompt and efficient delivery of these services by the front line staff. To ensure quick delivery of these services, banks have to introduce revolutionary technological changes like Electronic Fund Transfer, Electronic Clearing Service, Net Working the Service Branches, Automatic teller Machines, modern and up-dated communication facilities.

Barahmandam and Narayanan (1990), Chandhuri (1981), Gupta and Bansal (1994), Nageswar (1987), Saxeena (1988) and Srivastava (1994) have, in their studies, highlighted opening and closing of bank accounts, time taken for issue and encashment of cheques and drafts, collection of instruments drawn on outstation centers, delay in credit of telephonic transfer remittances and postings of pass books as areas which need careful attention by banks in order to reduce growing customer dissatisfaction. They have also stressed that customer dissatisfaction persists because instructions issued by head offices of banks did not percolate to the gross root level functionaries and the later did not have the same concern in the matter of public accountability as at the corporate level. In an attempt to overcome the growing customer dissatisfaction, several researchers (Harsh, 1993; Muniraj, 1994; Nageswar, 1987; Sundaram, 1984; and Tandam and Sanjay, 1994) have emphasized training and development of bank personnel, employee motivation, procedures and systems, customer education, analysis of individual customer behaviour which implies the banker to have training in psychological and social aspects, opening of extra counters on busy days (pay days, examination fee pay days etc.) and display of day to day changes in rules and regulations which will improve understanding between both bank staff and its customers.

To sum up, banks in order to remain competitive should aim at customer satisfaction as the main purpose of banking is, "to create and deliver customer needed service in a customer satisfying manner (Talwar Committee Observation). This depends upon two important elements, viz., creation and delivery of prompt, effective, qualitative and suitable customer services. Creation of wide range of services, making them suitable to customer needs and convenient through implementation of better technology, introduction of creative and new schemes. Prompt, accurate, quick, convenient and courteous delivery of these services is possible through better HRD practices, which aim at grooming employees particularly front line staff.

Banking Technology

Financial reforms had its impact on Indian banks and financial institutions. In the fast changing financial environment, fierce competition and changes in the regulatory policies created uncertainty and risk for the Indian banking industry. Realising this fact, academicians and practitioners highlighted, in their studies, that information source in banks is of capital importance and they look at information technology as strategic response to changing financial environment/ challenges (Ammayya 1996; Naidu 1997; Saraf, 1997; Salma, 1998). The Rangarajan Committee Report (1989) was the first path breaking step in this direction, which highlighted that computerization must be looked upon as a means to improve customer service and efficiency and that the banks' workforce should realize that mechanization would lead to growth and employment expansion (Bide, 1997). Subsequently, Narasimham Committee (1992), while highlighting the problems faced by Indian public sector banks, and, as an antidote to the identified lacunae, also stressed the need for greater measure of computerization in banks. The committee observed that modern banking involves a great deal of processing of mass of information and commitment to technology is the only solution that ensures timeliness, accuracy and resultant improved performance and enhanced customer service (Bide, 1997). On similar lines, several academicians and practitioners argued that technology in banks would help to increase the level of productivity and customer satisfaction (Girish and Preetha, 1997; Kirandikar, 1999; Middleton, 1994; Nageswar and Pramod, 1990; Nageswar, 1987; and Vijaya 1991). To meet the challenges posed by the entry of foreign banks, Indian banks will have to invest heavily in technology to meet competition, reduce cost, improve customer service, improve productivity and offer new products/services.

Technology in service organizations is a must for success. Shed the archaic, myopic outlook and be open to modern technology in marketing your services are the views shared by many scholars. These scholars have studied technology in service organizations from different perspectives. Harsh (1993) studied beneficial aspects of technology and identified five major benefits of technology to a service organisation. First, the equipment could be employed in place of work force. Such substitution of equipment and machines for labour reduce cost of operation and increase efficiency. Second, introduction of technology may help achieve standardization in the quality of service. Third, higher service levels could be achieved by such blending of technology. Fourth, service organisations can maintain close links with their customers by hooking up in the computer net works. Such technologies permit one firm to link itself with the information system of the other and, thereby, be in touch. Finally, technology may be useful in directing employees' behaviour and enhance status and motivation.

Ammayya (1996), along with Godse (1997) and Naidu (1997), while appreciating the introduction of information technology in banks, stressed on training needs of people who play crucial role in turning the hardware and software and networking tools into a powerful combination to aid the banks in improving the service quality and performance. Srivastava (1997) also studied technology in banks and the training needs of employees but pointed out problems in training to such technical personnel. This is because unlike other areas like credit and foreign exchange, it is not only the personnel posted in banking technology departments who are to be trained and retrained, but also training has to be provided to the user system, i.e. operational executives and staff. The author suggests training to technology oriented staff in communication, interpersonal skills, team building and leadership qualities, which they are usually lacking.

Salma (1998) studied technological reforms in the banking sector. The emphasis on technology as the key factor for improving performance and increasing productivity in banks has been well exemplified by her through illustrations. Most Indian banks, mainly private ones, are hastening to interconnect their countrywide branches (Aishah, 1997). Budgetary spending on technology is increasing (Salma, 1998). Keeping on the lines of promoting speed, SBI has introduced Electronic Fund Transfer Systems (EFTS) in thirty branches in sixteen cities in two schemes, State Bank Instant Remittance (SBIR) and State Bank Rapid Remittance (SBRR) when remittance are made the same and the next day respectively (Shanker, 1995). Jha (2000), in his study, while highlighting the use of technology, identified latest developments in banking technology such as Electronic Fund Transfer System, Direct Deposit Pay Roll, Point of Sales System, Credit and Debit Cards, Pre-authorized Transfer, Automated Clearing Houses etc. In the area of electronic banking, credit deposit machine is a latest chapter. Jha (2000) also believes that management of information, with the help of new generation of information technology, will increase decision-making capacity of professional and delivery capacity of front line staff.

Many authors, while studying customer service and bank marketing, have observed that the need for computerization/ bank automation has arisen because customers expect their cheques to be encashed within a reasonable time, prompt realization of clearing cheques, a quick transfer of funds and timely receipt of correct statements of their accounts etc (Chidambaram and Alamelu, 1996; Muniraj, 1994; Nageswar and Pramod, 1990; Satya, 1984; and Vajaya, 1991). All this can be possible if banks are automated. Unlike private and foreign banks, public sector banks, in India, have legacy of excess manpower (Dipankar, 1995) high NPAs (Srinivasa, 1996) or old systems and procedures to follow which resulted in the drop of market share from 91% in 1991 to 79% in April 1999 (out of which SBI and its subsidiaries cover 25%) and also most of the time good corporate customers are lost to competitors (Karandikar, 1999). Karandikar in his study observed that the dividing lines between commercial banks, development banks, mutual funds, insurance companies and other financial institutions are getting thinner and thinner and suggests total bank automation for public sector banks, if they want to survive, grow and make profit or even provide continuity of jobs to their employees.

To sum up, the adoption of technology in banks is increasing with the growing use of Internet, electronic commerce, and various other banking innovations. Evolution of technology in banks is taking place at an enormous pace and it is only question of time before banks commit themselves on full-scale technology upgradation, aiding their growth and adding to their competitive might. The computer and the communication age is opening up a flood of new opportunities that are redefining the very concept of traditional banking. It is for the individual banks to reinvest themselves and reconfigure their business processes and practices in tune with the growing customer expectations in an ever increasing competitive environment. There is no way, a bank can remain lukewarm to new technology products and yet hope to grow because it is a choice of survival or extinction. Technology, if properly implemented, after strategic considerations, provides a level playing field in a global environment.

Research Gaps and the Agenda for Future Research

The above review highlights some important studies on

service quality, customer services and banking technology and brings to light the gaps and deficiencies in the respective areas. It conveys that in developed countries a good deal of effort has already been made to study a large number of problems associated with service quality. In India, unfortunately, little attention has been paid to study such problems. This may be due to the fact that services marketing in general and service quality in particular, till recently, was not recognized as an area of significance in the socio-economic requirements of our country. Most of the existing studies are by their nature, general and descriptive and lack empirical evidence. With a view to study service quality, with an objective and analytical approach, all the problems inhibiting the growth of research in the field will have first to be looked into.

Services marketing in general and service quality in particular cannot be understood without due reference to the shades of Babakus and Boller, Bolton and Drew, Carman, Brown and Swartz, Carson and Gilmore, Gronroos, Lehtinan and Lehtinan, Parasuraman, at.el., and Zeithaml and Berry. The roots of the service quality research lie in early conceptual framework from Europe (e.g. Gronroos, 1983; Lehtinan and Lehtinan, 1982). Most of the recent work on service quality in marketing can be credited to the pioneering and continuing contributions of A. Parasuraman, Leonard Barry and Valarie Zeithaml.

In a liberalized environment an analysis of service quality in banks, in the context of socio-economic transformation of an economy has a vital significance, but in India, unfortunately, it was almost left out of in-depth analysis. The dynamic process of development coupled with structural, financial and technological changes have given birth to tough competition not only from banks but also from non-banking institutions. In view of these developments, there is a need to study quality of existing and new financial services, bank customer relationship, service technology and various other issues so as to meet growing needs of customers and bankers. These are immediate tasks awaiting further in-depth study and research. The application of 'SERVQUAL' propounded by Paransuraman, et al. (1985, 1988) to measure service quality was yet to be tested though it has been widely used in a number of service organisations in developed countries.

Very little effort has so far been made to assess and develop the concepts, research methods and procedures used in research on service quality. The present methods of assessing service quality in banks is quite unsatisfactory as most of the research is descriptive in nature and deals with the problems of bank customers in transacting with bank branches, the extent of customer satisfaction, indifference of staff towards customers etc. Other vital issues such as physical facilities available in a branch, branch automation, convenient location, convenient banking hours, bank customer relationship, service delivery, friendly staff which have a direct bearing on service quality have rarely been touched with any empirical evidence. This calls for well-organized research and documentation centers, which are indispensable for the growth of bank marketing.

In conclusion, with a view to strengthen the analytical framework for studies in service quality, it is desirable to concentrate the research efforts in the above-mentioned areas. In addition to these significant areas of research, the following form the other fruitful and revealing areas of research as time is over due to focus attention on them.

1. The forces of deregulation, technology and customer care are broadly likely to have an impact on bank marketing. There is a need to study how technology can help to bring efficiency in banking culture, to retain existing customers and how it can be helpful

in increasing productivity, profitability and customer service.

2. Delivering consistently good service quality is difficult but profitable for service organizations. Customer service centers around two important aspects, viz., designing of a service and delivery of service. Both aspects are equally important, because bad delivery of a perfectly designed service is as harmful as perfect delivery of a badly designed service. There is need to identify and investigate those potential factors which affect the delivery of quality service.
3. Service firms face many critical problems as they differ in intangibility inseparability, perishability and heterogeneity from goods firms. What are these problems? How are they changing due to environmental, competitive, and other conditions? The services marketing research needs to focus on the most critical problems facing service firms if it is to be of maximum value.
4. Fluctuation of demand in service organisations is the most troublesome issue and seems to be the most fertile area for future research.
5. Relationship marketing, an emerging concept, is gaining wider acceptability in service organisations. The cost of maintaining/continuing existing relationships compared to developing of new customers needs a fresh look to reveal the benefits of relationship marketing.
6. Relationship between productivity, quality, cost reduction, technology, overall socio-economic development and banking services.

7. Evolving a system of bank marketing based on trust, openness of communication, word of mouth communication that is critical, as services are intangible and heterogeneous in nature and participative involvement of parties.
8. The employees are in many senses an important part of service product. They represent the fifth 'p' in the services marketing mix. Therefore, there is a need to study/investigate internal marketing because their participation and role is recognized as being critical to levels of service quality and service delivery.

3

Research Methodology

In line with the objectives of the study, this chapter discusses SERVQUAL model used for studying service quality followed by research design of the study including universe of the study, the sample size and structure, data collection, data analysis, research methods and at the end identifies limitations of the study.

The SERVQUAL Model

As the race to compete and survive intensifies, business firms discover their service offerings becoming dangerously similar to one another (e.g., service products of airlines, banks, fast food and the like equally measure up to one another's specifications). The only thing that differentiates them from one another is the quality of service they offer to their customers. Quality, therefore, has become an issue of major concern to most service organisations due to increasing threat of competition. Indeed several authors (Buzzell and Wiersema, 1981; Garvin, 1983; Gronroos, 1982; Leonard and Sasser, 1982; Lewis and Booms, 1983; Schoeffler, Buzzell and Heany, 1974; Takenchi and Quelch, 1983; Zeithaml, Parasuraman and Berry, 1985 to mention a few) argue that quality has a direct bearing on a company's performance and future growth.

Success with regard to service quality has traditionally been assessed by measurement of customer satisfaction.

However, as the literature has evolved, service quality has come to be defined in terms of the difference between customer expectations and perceptions. Expectations are desires or wants, what people feel a service provider should offer, and are formed on the basis of previous experience of a company and all the elements of its marketing mix (which include process, people and physical evidence (Boom and Bitner, 1981), competition and word-of-mouth communication. Perceptions are consumer judgements about actual service performance/delivery by a company and so, if there is a short fall in the comparison between predicted and perceived service, then a service "gap" exists which providers would wish to close. The consumer service quality gap is influenced by other four gaps or short falls which were identified from the extensive research of Parasuraman, et al., (1985, 1988). These gaps relate to management assessment of consumer needs, development of service systems, employees involvement in service delivery, and external communications about service delivery.

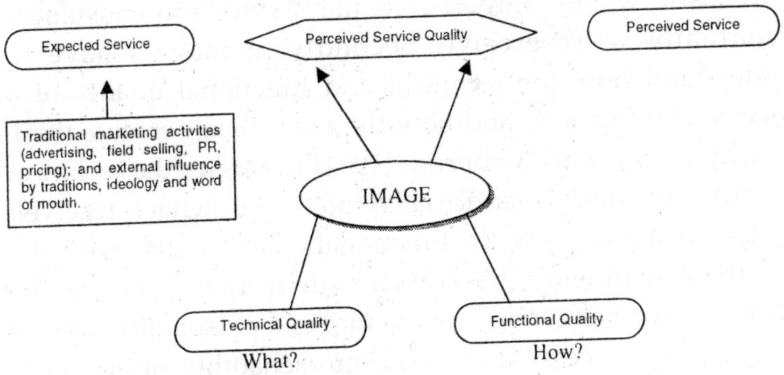

Figure 1: THE SERVICE QUALITY MODEL

Source: Gronroos Christian (1984) "A Service Quality Model and Its Marketing Implications", European Journal of Marketing, Vol. 18, No. 4, pp. 36-44.

However, before Parasuraman, et al. (1985), Gronroos (1984) proposed that service firms, in order to compete successfully, must develop quality of their service and they must first define how service quality is perceived by the consumers and secondly, determine in what way service quality is influenced (Fig.1). Gronroos suggested that functional quality is more important dimension of perceived service than the technical quality. Therefore, essence of effectiveness in managing services lies in improving the functional quality of a firm's service by managing the buyer-seller interaction (interactive marketing) than the traditional marketing activities.

Managing the perceived quality of service means that one has to match the expected service and the perceived service to each other so that customer satisfaction is achieved. To keep the gap between expected and perceived service minimal two things are critical. First, the promises about how the service will perform given by traditional marketing activities and communicated by word-of-mouth, must not be unrealistic when compared to the service the consumers eventually will perceive. Secondly, managers have to understand how the technical and functional quality of a service is influenced and how the customers perceive these quality dimensions. Gronross (1984) discusses the technical quality (outcome) of service encounters – i.e., what is received by the customer – and the functional quality of the process – i.e., the way in which the service is delivered, to include the attitudes and behaviour, appearance and personality, service mindedness, accessibility and approachability of customer contact personnel – together with corporate image dimension of quality.

In order to develop greater understanding of the nature of service quality and how it is achieved in an organisation, a service quality model (figure 2) and a measurement instrument, SERVQUAL (see appendices I & II) for assessing service quality has been developed by Parasuraman, et. al. (1985, 1988). Their model clearly indicates that consumer's quality perceptions are influenced by a service of five distinct gaps occurring in organisations. These gaps, on the service provider's side, which can impede delivery of services that consumers perceive to be of high quality, are:

Gap-1: Difference between consumer expectations and management perceptions of consumer expectations.

Gap-2: Difference between management perceptions of consumer expectations and service quality specifications.

Gap-3: Difference between service quality specifications and the service actually delivered.

Gap-4: Difference between service delivery and what is communicated about the service to consumers.

Gap-5: Difference between the perceived service and expected service. This gap depends on the size and direction of the four gaps associated with the delivery of service quality.

The foundation and focus of this model lay in identifying the key components of service quality namely, customer expectations and perceptions and the service delivery associated with these. The basic premise of the model was that there exists a 'gap' between customer expectations and perceptions and the actual delivery of the service. In an attempt to measure service quality they identified ten dimensions, which they then reduced to five to form the core of the SERVQUAL measuring instrument. The five final dimensions chosen were:

Tangibility: The appearance of physical facilities, equipment, personnel and communication materials.

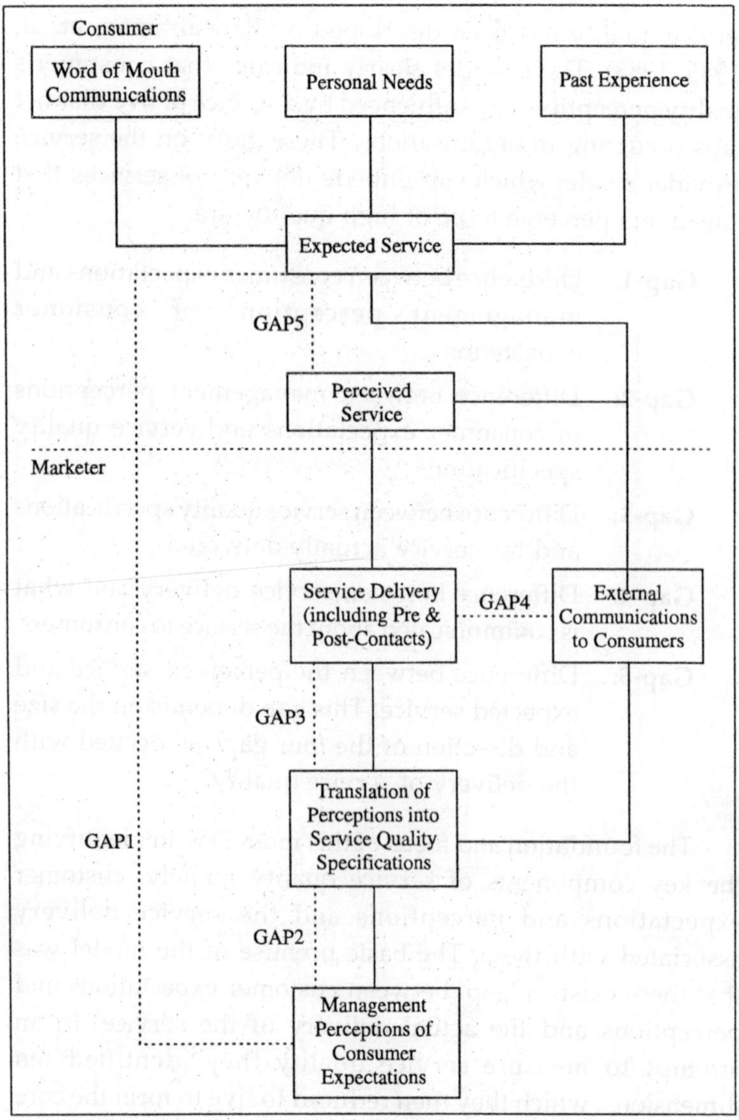

Figure 2: CONCEPTUAL MODEL OF SERVICE QUALITY

Source: Parasuraman A., Zeithaml Valarie A., and Leonard L. Berry (1985) "A Conceptual Model of Service Quality and its Implications For Future Research", Journal of Marketing, Vol. 49, pp. 41-50.

Reliability: The ability to perform promised service dependably and accurately.

Responsiveness: The willingness to help customers and provide prompt service.

Assurance: The knowledge and courtesy of employees and their ability to convey trust and confidence.

Empathy: The caring individualized attention provided to the customer.

These are then measured using twenty-two items (SERVQUAL) with respondents first giving their expectations of service and then their evaluation of the actual service. Satisfaction is calculated as the difference between perceptions and expectations (each item weighted according to its importance). Parasuraman et al. (1988) established that a mismatch between expectations and perceptions causes dissatisfaction, a 'performance gap' as they call it. As found with other writers the process of service delivery was considered to be a key feature in the assessment of quality (Cronin and Taylor, 1992, 1994; Liljandar and Strandrik, 1994).

Gronross (1990) and Gilmore and Carson (1993) also identified the possible occurance of performance gaps and in each case attribute the gap to a failure by marketing managers to balance the marketing mix in order that customers are led to expect more than the organisation can offer.

The next work of the same team of researchers (Parasuraman et al., 1991) identified an exhaustive set of constructs that could affect the magnitude and direction of Gap 4. Most of these construct involved communication and control processes used to manage employees, as well as consequences of these processes. Figure 3 is an extended model of service quality summarising the various organisational constructs affecting the gaps.

They summarised by stating that the service quality is a subjective assessment that customers arrive at by comparing the service level they believe an organisation ought to deliver to the service level they perceive is being delivered. Extensive qualitative research conducted by Parasuraman, et al. (1991) suggests that service quality deficiencies perceived by customers, i.e., the gap between their expectations and perceptions, are caused by a series of organisational gaps.

- Marketing Information Gap: inadequate or inaccurate management understanding of customer's service expectations.
- Standards Gap: management's failure to develop performance specifications reflecting customer's expectations.
- Service Performance Gap: discrepancy between service performance specification and service actually delivered.
- Communication Gap: discrepancy between communications to customers describing the service and the service actually delivered.

Parasuraman, et al. (1985) conceptual SERVQUAL model was taken up by many researchers. Research using the model can be grouped into two broad aspects. Primarily, the widening of the scope of service situations, mostly industry specific, by using the model for empirical research into measuring service quality in a specific industry. A secondary, but equally important, aspect centered on the issue of 'quality' and how to increase customer satisfaction by improving the quality of a service.

Thus the comparison of customer expectations with their perceptions of a service became the major focus of attention in the measurement of service quality from the early 1980s until the present day. Examples of the widening and use of

SERVQUAL are many and varied (see, for example, Lewis (1987), hotel services; Brown and Swartz (1989), medical services; Carman (1990), car retailing; Lewis (1991), service quality in banks; Fick and Ritchie (1991), travel and tourism; Saleh and Ryan (1991), hotels; Johns (1993), hospitality; Young et al. (1994), American airline industry).

The above research findings provide enough scope and justification of the validity of SERVQUAL instrument. The numerous examples of industry-specific empirical studies using SERVQUAL was, therefore, chosen as an ideal instrument for studying service quality in banks.

Parasuraman, et al. (1985), model is build upon the premise that although quality in tangible goods had previously been described and measured by marketers, quality in services had not. The conceptual model for service quality is presented as a result of an extensive exploratory investigation of quality in four service businesses. It is built upon the argument that quality is a comparison between expectations and performance and quality evaluations involve outcomes and processes. This study led to the identification of four gaps on the service provider's side that may affect service quality as perceived by the customer (with the fifth gap defined as the resulting difference between perceived and expected service).

Applications of SERVQUAL

SERVQUAL is a concise multiple item scale with good reliability and validity that companies, from a broad spectrum of services, can use to better understand the service expectations and perceptions of their customers. It provides a basic skeleton through its expectations/perceptions format encompassing statements for each of the five service quality dimensions. The instrument can be adapted or supplemented to fit the characteristics or specific research needs of a particular organisation.

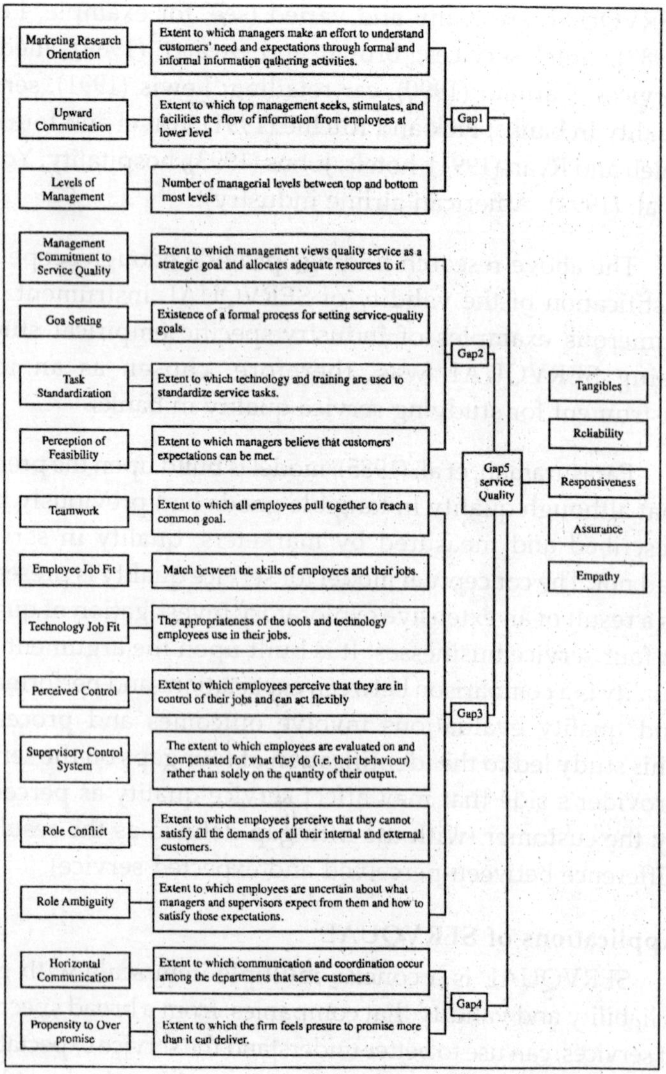

Figure 3: Extended Model of Service Quality

Source: A. Parasuraman, Leonard L. Berry and Valarie A. Zeithaml (1991), "Perceived Service Quality as a Customer Based Performance Measure: An Empirical Examination Using an Extended Service Quality Model", Human Resource Management, Fall., Vol. 3, pp. 335-364.

The data obtained from SERVQUAL instrument can be used to compute service quality gap scores at different levels in detail for each dimension, for each statement pair, or combined across all dimensions. By examining the various gap scores a company can not only assess its overall quality of service as perceived by customers but also identify the key dimensions, and facets within those dimensions on which it should focus its quality improvement efforts.

SERVQUAL can be used in a number of ways as follows:

1. SERVQUAL is most valuable when it is used periodically to track service quality trends over a period of time. Such a comparison reveals not only how the gap is changing but also whether the gap is changing because of changing expectations or due to changing perceptions, or both.
2. SERVQUAL instrument can also be used to determine the relative importance of the five dimensions of service quality in influencing customer's overall quality perceptions.
3. One very important potential application of SERVQUAL is its use in categorising a firm's customers into several perceived – quality segments (e.g., high, medium and low) on the basis of their individual SERVQUAL scores. These segments can be analysed on the basis of (1) demographic, psychographics and/or other profiles (2) the relative importance of five dimensions in influencing service quality perceptions and (3) the reasons behind the perceptions reported. This particular application of SERVQUAL makes it useful tool for segmentation and evaluation of those segments. The outputs of SERVQUAL can also be used to develop effective positioning strategies aimed at different segments.

4. SERVQUAL can also be used by multi-unit retail companies to track the level of service provided by each store in the chain. By asking respondents to indicate the particular store in the chain with which they are most familiar and to provide perception responses for that unit, the researcher can compare each store's average SERVQUAL score with the scores from other stores. Service quality scores can then be a factor in store manager performance appraisals and compensation, among other use. Also, SERVQUAL scores for the individual stores can be used to group outlets into several clusters with varying quality images. A careful examination of the characteristics of the stores in different clusters may reveal key attributes that facilitate – or hinder – the delivery of high quality service.
5. A company can also use SERVQUAL to assess its service performance relative to its principle competitors. The two-section format of the instrument, with separate expectation and perception sections, makes it convenient to measure the quality of several firms simply by including a set of perception statements for each firm. The expectations section does not have to be repeated for each firm. A company that uses SERVQUAL to identify the most salient service quality dimensions for its target markets, and to compare itself to the competitions in terms of strengths and weaknesses on these particular dimensions, will certainly have a sense of what its priorities should be with regard to service quality.

On the whole, SERVQUAL has a variety of potential applications. It can help a wide range of service and retailing organisations in assessing consumer expectations about and perceptions of service quality. It can also help in pinpointing areas requiring managerial attention and action to improve service quality. The various applications of SERVQUAL make it a truly versatile and indispensable tool for successful service marketers.

Universe of the Study

The study seeks to study service quality in banks in Northern India, which include J&K State, Punjab, Haryana and Delhi. However, the survey was confined to urban areas only keeping in view the concentration of banks in these areas as well as the paucity of time and financial resources of the researcher.

The study is further limited to five banks in Northern India, namely State Bank of India (SBI)*, Punjab National Bank (PNB)*, Jammu and Kashmir Bank (JKB)*, City Bank (CB)* and Standard Chartered Grindlays Bank (SCGB)*. These banks were purposely selected for the present study keeping in view their role and involvement in shaping the economic destiny and in instrumentalising the process of social and economic transformation in Northern India. Specifically, in terms of advancing credit and deposits, employee strength and branch network, they stand at the top. The following Table 3.1 clearly justifies the selection rationale of these five banks.

Further, customers of any bank are largely classified into three categories as follows:

- Retail clientele
- Corporate clientele
- Correspondent Bank clientele

TABLE 3.1

Bank Business, Employees, Branches as on March 2002

Banks	*Rupees in Crores*			*Total*	*Total*
	Deposits	*Advances*	*Total*	*Employees*	*Branches*
State Bank of India Group	3,12,118	3,045	3,15,163	2,91,199	13,561
State Bank of India	2,42,828 (77.8)	2,593 (85.15)	2,45,421 (77.87)	2,14,845 (73.77)	9,078 (66.94)
Nationalised Banks	5,47,259	7,411	5,54,670	5,06,612	32,757
Punjab National Bank	56,131 (10.25)	724 (9.76)	56,855 (10.25)	58,309 (11.50)	3,879 (11.84)
Private Sector Banks	1,36,667	3,469	1,40,136	69,073	5,233
Jammu and Kashmir Bank	11,168 (8.17)	131 (3.77)	11,299 (8.06)	6,470 (9.36)	426 (8.14)
Foreign Banks	59,190	2,284	61,474	14,205	190
City Bank	14,052 (23.74)	503 (22.02)	14,555 (23.67)	1,476 (10.39)	15 (7.89)
Standard Chartered Gridlays Bank	8,256 (13.94)	436 (19.08)	8,692 (14.13)	3,122 (21.97)	41 (21.57)
All scheduled Commercial Banks	10,55,234	16,209	10,71,443	8,81,089	51,741

Note: *Figures within parentheses are percentages to total.*

Source: *IBA Bulletin (Special Issue) March, 2002, Vol. xxiv, No. 3, pp. 264-299.*

* Because of frequent references to these banks in the study, hereafter their abbreviations as given in brackets are used.

The services sought by retail customers (i.e., individuals) are savings/current accounts, chequebook facility, outstanding orders, remittances and term deposits besides lending products to cover vehicle/housing/other loans. This retail banking constitutes nearly eighty per cent of the total banking business (Srivastava, 1994). In view of this fact, the present study is limited to retail banking only.

The Sample and Sampling Design

i)Bank Sample

Two public sector banks, one private bank and two foreign banks were selected for the in-depth study. In total three hundred seventy bank officials of the sample organisations, were approached by the scholar to fill up the SERVQUAL instrument with a view to measure the perceptions about service quality they are delivering to their respective customers. Table 3.2 provides details about the number of bank officials that were interviewed. While choosing bank officials, the method of convenience sampling was used. All other important factors about bank officials like age, level of education, scale of pay and location of bank were taken into consideration while approaching the bank official.

TABLE 3.2

Total Bank Officials Interviewed/Contacted

Banks	*Bank Customers*	*Percentage*
SBI	99	27
PNB	101	27
JKB	101	27
CB	29	8
SCGB	40	11
Total	370	100

Note: *Figures within parentheses are percentages to total.*

ii)Customers Sample

The present study is based upon the experiences and opinions expressed by bank customers regarding their expectations and perceptions about the quality of service they are receiving from their respective banks. For this purpose, a sample of eight hundred bank customers was taken from sample organization. Table 3.3 shows that 50% bank customers that were interviewed are from nationalised banks, 25% from private banks, while as the remaining 25% are from foreign banks. Again, while choosing a bank customer for present study, the method of simple random sampling was used. All important demographic characteristics like age, level of education, level of income, profession and geographic location of the bank were taken into consideration while choosing bank customers. All these characteristics have an important bearing upon bank customers' evaluation (regarding expectations and perceptions) of service quality. The effort was made to give a balanced representation to above demographic characteristics to make the sample representative.

TABLE 3.3

Total Bank Customers Interviewed

Banks	*Bank Customers*	*Percentage*
SBI	197	25
PNB	201	25
JKB	199	25
CB	99	12
SCGB	104	13
Total	800	100

Note: *Figures within parentheses are percentages to total.*

Data Collection

The study is based both on primary data and secondary data. The major part of the study, however, is based on primary data collected from bank officials and bank customers through SERVQUAL instrument. The major objective of the primary data collected from respective bank customers was to study customer expectations and perceptions about service quality they are receiving from their banks. While as the opinion expressed by bank officials on said SERVQUAL instrument gave an assessment whether banks meet the expectations of their customers, or they are below or exceed the expectations of their customers as far as delivering quality of service is concerned. The SERVQUAL instrument also covered the opinions of both bank officials and bank customers regarding levels of importance to service quality dimensions. Thus, an attempt was made to make a comparative study among bank officials and bank customers as far as levels of importance of service quality dimensions are concerned. The data was collected personally by visiting branches of various banks selected for the study.

In order to seek fair and frank responses on quality of service in banks, both from bank respondents and bank officials, the importance of service quality (to customers and bank officials), alternatives on offer to customers, knowledge of costs and benefits of keeping customers relative to attracting new ones, company's performance and future growth used to be discussed first.

Data Analysis

(I)Bank Officials

The demographic profile of bank officials has been given in Table 3.4. With a view to seek balanced opinion from bank officials regarding the quality of services they are delivering to respective customers, the effort was made to give due representation to most of the demographic characteristics to make the sample representative.

Table 3.4 clearly reveals that vital demographic characteristics of bank officials such as age, level of education, scale of pay, geographic location of bank official have been considered while seeking their opinion regarding service quality.

TABLE 3.4

Demographic Profile of Bank Officials

Demographic Characteristics		*BANKS*				
		SBI	*PNB*	*JKB*	*CB*	*SCGB*
Age in years	20 – 35	10 (10)	11 (11)	5 (5)	4 (14)	5 (13)
	35 – 50	70 (71)	66 (65)	89 (87)	25 (86)	29 (72)
	Above 50	19 (19)	24 (24)	07 (8)	— —	6 (15)
	Bachelors Degree/ Diploma	50 (51)	38 (38)	50 (49)	4 (14)	8 (20)
Level of Education	P.G. Degree/ Diploma	35 (35)	48 (47)	44 (44)	22 (76)	24 (60)
	Professional/ Technical	11 (11)	13 (13)	06 (06)	03 (10)	08 (20)
	Higher Studies	03 (13)	02 (02)	01 (01)	—	—
	1st	41 (42)	26 (26)	33 (33)	01 (03)	01 (03)
Scale of	2nd	23 (23)	42 (41)	35 (34)	10 (35)	11 (27)
Pay	3rd	33 (33)	32 (32)	22 (22)	12 (42)	18 (45)
	4th	01 (01)	01 (01)	10 (10)	05 (17)	09 (22)
	5th	01 (01)	— —	01 (01)	01 (03)	01 (31)
Location of Bank	J&K State	20 (20)	21 (21)	65 (64)	— —	06 (15)
	Punjab	59 (60)	60 (59)	15 (15)	— —	10 (25)
	Delhi	20 (20)	20 (20)	21 (21)	29 (100)	24 (60)

Note: Figures within parenthesis are percentages to total.

(II) Bank Customers

Table 3.5 highlights the demographic characteristics of bank customers. In order to seek balanced opinion regarding customer expectations and perceptions about service quality in banks, respondents bearing varied demographic characteristics were randomly selected for the present study. Table 3.5 clearly reveals that vital demographic characteristics such as age, level of education, level of income, geographic location of respondents and profession have been considered while seeking the opinion regarding service quality expectations and perceptions. In particular, the level of education, income and profession provided meaningful variation about respondents' expectations and perceptions. Level of banking competition in different regions emerged vital demographic character on which expectations and perceptions vary considerably.

TABLE 3.5

Demographic Profile of Bank Customers

Demographic Characteristics		*BANKS*				
		SBI	*PNB*	*JKB*	*CB*	*SCGB*
Age in years	20 – 35	31 (16)	29 (14)	58 (29)	19 (19)	20 (19)
	35 – 50	101 (51)	107 (54)	100 (50)	64 (65)	65 (63)
	Above 50	65 (33)	65 (32)	41 (21)	16 (16)	19 (18)
Level of Education	Bachelors Degree/ Diploma	108 (55)	108 (54)	95 (48)	19 (19)	29 (28)
	P.G. Degree/ Diploma	74 (37)	77 (38)	81 (41)	65 (66)	63 (60)
	Professional/ Technical	15 (108)	10 (05)	17 (08)	15 (15)	08 (08)
	Higher Studies	——	06 (03)	06 (03)	——	04 (04)
Level of Income per month (Rs.)	5,000 – 15,000	46 (23)	53 (26)	78 (39)	17 (17)	16 (15)
	15,000 – 25,000	81 (41)	49 (25)	58 (29)	30 (31)	35 (34)
	25,000 – 35,000	35 (18)	55 (27)	31 (16)	27 (27)	28 (27)
	Above 35,000	35 (18)	44 (22)	32 (16)	25 (25)	25 (24)
Location of Bank	J&K State	44 (22)	46 (23)	145 (73)	——	18 (17)
	Punjab	123 (63)	128 (64)	25 (12)	——	35 (34)
	Delhi	30 (15)	27 (13)	29 (15)	99 (100)	51 (49)
Profession	Business	86 (44)	117 (58)	93 (47)	60 (61)	55 (53)
	Service	111 (56)	84 (42)	106 (53)	39 (39)	49 (47)

Note: Figures within parenthesis are percentages to total.

Statistical Techniques Used

In order to sharpen the inferences drawn, the interpretation of data has been made on the basis of simple frequencies and means. Weighted average scores have also been calculated to study levels of importance to service quality dimensions. T. Test has been performed to study level of significance between customer perceptions and expectations. T. Test was also helpful in studying significance levels regarding service quality among different banks. One-way ANOVA has been calculated to study variation in service quality among banks, under study.

Limitations of the Study

The study was primarily based on a survey in Northern India conducted with the help of SERVQUAL instrument. It is entirely based on the views and opinions expressed by the respondents. The accuracy and authenticity of the study depends upon the truthfulness of the revelations of bank customers and bank officials. The results cannot be accurate if the respondents keep away from speaking the truth. Some other limitations of the study are as follows:

- Some bank respondents who are mostly less educated do not know their rights as bank customers. They prefer to suffer in silence rather than raise their voice against poor services, if provided, cannot give fair opinion about quality of service in banks.
- The present study was limited tc urban areas in Northern India due to paucity of time and financial resources. One of the limitations of the study is that the opinion of rural customers regarding service quality in banks could not be studied.
- The level of banking competition in a particular region gives rise to expectations. Banking competition varies considerably in Northern India

and as a result a bank respondent or bank official who is not exposed to competitive banking environment cannot give balanced opinion about quality of service in banks.

- Some bank officials, in order to play safe, might have not provided correct assessment about the quality of service they are delivering to their respective customers. Also being busy in routine work they might have filled up the questionnaire quickly, which leaves enough scope for incorrect assessment about services in their banks.

However, care has been taken to exclude those questionnaires for analysis purpose which appeared misleading so as to present balanced picture about the quality of service among the sample organisations.

4

Service Quality in Banks

This chapter presents the empirical fiendings of the study regarding service quality among banking organisations in Northern India. It also discusses service quality variation across demographic variables among the sample organisations besides a comparison between banks and respective bank customers regarding levels of importance to service quality dimensions.

Introduction

One of the major objectives of the study was to study/ measure service quality and its dimensions in banks, under study, through SERVQUAL scale. To achieve this objective, the first question was directed at the measurement of service quality construct. Two equations of service quality (SERVQUAL, equation 1; weighted SERVQUAL, equation 2nd) construct were used for the present study as follows:

Service Quality: (performance-Expectations)-I.

Service Quality: Importance (performance-Expectations)-II

Service Quality: (performance)-III

Service Quality: Importance (performance)-IV

Both the equation (equation I and II) provide strong research support for measuring/studying service quality of an organisation. The research findings of Gronroos, (1982), Lehtinen and Lehtinen, (1983), Zeithaml, et al., (1991), Sasser, et al., (1978) and the extensive focus group interviews conducted by Parasuraman, et al., (1985) unambiguously support the notion that service quality, as perceived by consumers, stems from a comparison of what they feel service firms should offer (i.e., from their expectations) with their perceptions of what they actually offer. Service quality, therefore, is the degree and direction of the discrepancy between consumers' perceptions and expectations. Moreover, information generated by this approach (equation I) has greater diagnostic value. Equation II, however, has been recommended by the SERVQUAL developers (Parasuraman at el., 1994) to define/measure overall service quality of an organisation. The remaining two equations (III and IV) have little research evidence as constructs for measuring service quality as reported by Parasuraman, et al., (1994).

Dimension-wise Analysis of Service Quality in Banks

As stated above, equation 1st has been used to measure service equality of banks, under study. For this purpose, mean perceptions and mean expectations of customers of sample organisation were computed. SERVQUAL score (service quality) were obtained by subtracting mean perceptions from mean expectations for each of the service quality dimension as reported in table 4.1 to 4.6. Each table provides information on all dimensions of service quality.

Tangibility

It is evident from table 4.1 that SERVQUAL score of CB followed by SCGB figures high on tangibility while as SBI followed by PNB figures low on the said dimension. The JKB is, however, in between the two extremes on this dimension. The element wise analysis of tangibility reveals that CB figures high as far as neatness of employees, communication material, physical facilities and up-to-date equipment's are concerned in comparison to other banks. All Indian banks figures low on SERVQUAL score as far as physical facilities and up-to-date equipment's available in a bank are concerned.

Table 4.1 clearly reveals severe deficiency in tangibles particularly in physical facilities and up-to-date equipments among Indian banks especially public sector banks. This finding suggests substantial investment on tangibles for Indian banks, which will improve service quality to a great extent. Tangibles particularly computerization of banking operations, internet and intranet based services, ATM etc., will take care of most of retail banking which constitutes eighty per cent of the total banking business. This will reduce workload of front line staff and will provide a way to quick response. This observation is in line with the Rangarajan Committee (1989) report, which stressed mechanization of Indian banking industry. The Committee had rightly commented that when banks are in tough competition with other financial intermediaries that are fully equipped and automated, there is a need for a greater measure of computerization. It pointed out that for the Indian banking system to be more competitive internally and to remain in step with wide ranging innovations taking place in industry abroad, a radical change in work technology is imperative (Bide, 1997). Many authors and practitioners have suggested banking technology as a means to improve customer services (Ammyya, 1996; Godse, 1997; Middleton, 1994; Saraf, 1997). The technological advancement, the world over, is so rapid and widespread that isolating banking and technology from each other is relatively an impossible preposition in today's fast changing competitive environment. Sesha Sai (1999) along with Mankidy (2000) while recommending the need for banking technology have raised HR issues which need to be addressed through relevant educational/training colleges. Table 4.1 highlights that public sector banks (SBI followed by PNB) figure too low on SERVQUAL score as far as physical facilities and up-to-date equipments are concerned as compared to foreign banks. Foreign banks, having technological edge, have expectedly scored high on tangibles and any further investment on said dimension will be waste of resources. Lakshmi (1991) in an empirical study reported that 73% of the respondents felt that the banks are being maintained in a good fashion is quite contrary as far as the findings of present study are concerned. In the said study, Lakshmi reported that forty-eight per cent respondents opined that the bank furnishing was just adequate and sixty three per cent of respondents felt that dressing was ordinary. Such a sad state of affairs has again come to the light when comparison is made between foreign banks and Indian banks as far as neatness of employees and physical facilities are concerned. Table 4.1 clearly reveals that Indian banks are lagging behind on tangibles as compared to foreign banks.

TABLE 4.1

Comparative SERVQUAL Scores of Banks on Tangibility

Elements of Service Quality (Tangibiity)	*BANKS*				
	SBI	*PNB*	*JKB*	*CB*	*SCGB*
1. Up-to-date equipment	-2.64	-2.41	-1.75	-0.33	-0.45
2. Physical facilities	-3.31	-2.83	-1.86	-0.31	-0.52
3. Employees are will dressed and neat appearing	-1.79	-1.52	-1.61	0.00	-0.27
4. Communication material	-1.84	-1.74	-1.70	-0.01	-0.15
Tangibility	-9.58	-8.5	-6.92	-0.65	-1.39
Rank	**5**	**4**	**3**	**1**	**2**

Reliability

The data in Table 4.2 highlights that SCGB followed by CB are high on reliability while as JKB followed by SBI are low on said dimension. The element-wise analysis of reliability reveals that all banks keep correct records of the transactions of their customers, though JKBs' position on this element is slightly low. The minor variation in SERVQUAL scores of foreign banks reveals that these banks are doing well on all elements of reliability. The low SERVQUAL scores of Indian banks, especially JKB (-1.51 and -1.48), reveals that these banks are poor as far as keeping promise and performance of service at promised time are concerned. PNB and SBI have more or less equal scores on all elements of reliability.

TABLE 4.2

Comparative SERVQUAL Scores of Banks on Reliability

Elements of Service Quality (Reliability)	*BANKS*				
	SBI	*PNB*	*JKB*	*CB*	*SCGB*
5. Promise to do something by a certain time, doing it.	-1.22	-1.13	-1.51	-0.32	-0.22
6. Being service in solving the problem	-1.19	-1.10	-1.42	-0.44	-0.21
7. Performing the service right the first time	-1.19	-1.09	-1.36	-0.23	-0.12
8. Providing the service at promised time	-1.14	-1.07	-1.48	-0.69	-0.36
9. Keeping records correctly	-0.48	-0.40	-0.94	-0.03	-0.02
Reliability	-5.22	-4.79	-6.71	-1.71	-0.93
Rank	**4**	**3**	**5**	**2**	**1**

Table 4.2 reveals that foreign banks figure high on reliability while as JKB followed by SBI figures low on said dimension. The element wise analysis of this dimension

highlights that Indian banks do not keep their promises. One of the reasons could be that Indian banks, under study, have more business to do as compared to foreign banks. Public sector banks including JKB operate in all segments, which increase the workload of frontline staff, and as such they fail to keep their promises. Foreign banks are operating in selected segments and as such have relatively less number of clients to attend. Further, they have a technological edge which takes care of most of their retail banking. As far as correct record keeping is concerned, foreign banks can expectedly exceed the expectations of their customers because of the said reason. Srivastava (1994) along with Brahmanandam and Narayana (1990) reported in their studies that banks do not start their operation at specified time, which results delays in transactions. Staff members usually report late by 15 to 30 minutes, while customers keep on waiting. Even while dealing with customers, they do not hesitate to leave their seats on some pretext or the other. The result is delay. The same sad state of affairs exists in banks, under study, because our banks lack positive work culture. Muniraj (1994) along with Ramachandra (1992) have similar observations about the work culture in banks and have recommended discipline as one of the marketing strategy to improve customer service. Srivastava (1994) in his study also confirms that only twenty per cent of the customers view the working conditions as appealing for business like transactions, rest eighty per cent are highly critical about it.

Responsiveness

From the analysis of data contained in Table 4.3, it is clear that foreign banks (SCGB followed by CB) figure high on responsiveness while as Indian Banks (SBI followed by PNB) figure low on said dimension. The elements-wise analysis of responsiveness highlights that SCGB meets the expectations of their customers as far as employees providing prompt service and employees willingness to help are concerned. The low negative score -0.28 and -0.29 of SCGB is highlighting this fact. High negative SERVQUAL score of SBI (-2.27) followed by PNB (-2.25) reveals the businesses of employees to respond to customer's request. Public sector bank's high negative SERVQUAL score reveals low service quality as far as responsiveness is concerned.

TABLE 4.3

Comparative SERVQUAL Scores of Banks on Responsiveness

Elements of Service Quality (Responsiveness)	*BANKS*				
	SBI	*PNB*	*JKB*	*CB*	*SCGB*
10. Telling customers exactly when service will be performed	-1.47	-1.19	-1.43	-0.42	-0.30
11. Employees providing prompt service to customers	-2.23	-2.03	-1.95	-0.68	-0.28
12. Employees who are always willing to help	-1.73	-1.60	-1.76	-0.53	-0.29
13. Employees who are never too busy to respond to customers requests	-2.27	-2.25	-1.66	-0.83	-0.42
Responsiveness	-7.70	-7.07	-6.8	-2.46	-1.29
Rank	**5**	**4**	**3**	**2**	**1**

Table 4.3 reveals that Indian banks, under study particularly SBI figure too low on responsiveness compared to foreign banks. Again lack of banking technology is the main contributing factor. This is evident from the two related elements of responsiveness, viz., employees providing prompt service and employees who are too busy to respond customers' requests wherein respondents of related banks have reported low perceptions regarding service quality. In the absence of

banking technology, the large volume of work results in delays (poor response) as employees are over busy with this work. However, Nageswar (1987) and Nageswar and Pramod (1990), in their studies, brought to light the fact that large corporate clients are able to get efficient and speedy service from their banks mainly because of the knowledge and efficiency of their own staff and the liaison with the banks, the small investors/ entrepreneurs are required to run to the banks for their work themselves. Since retail banking/personal banking constitutes eighty percent of the total banking business, which means that majority of bank customers face the problem of lack of concern from their respective banks. Foreign banks having technological edge are doing well on responsiveness dimension. Banking technology, which was absent during 90's, has increased customer aspirations today and as a result they expect quick response from their banks. Bhattacharyya and Ghose (1989), while highlighting urban bank saver's opinion, reported that only nine per cent clerks' are slow while as thirty nine per cent are very prompt and fifty two per cent usually prompt in providing services to customers. This state of affairs existed prior to 90's when we had controlled economy. Today customers will have a different perception on responsiveness of banks as they are in close competition with foreign banks, which are backed by sophisticated banking technology. The present study's findings are not in agreement with the views as reported by above mentioned scholars keeping in view the changed and competitive banking environments.

Assurance

The data in Table 4.4 reveals that SCGB followed by CB are high on assurance while as all Indian banks figure low on said dimension. The SERVQUAL score of all Indian banks under study on this dimension is nearly same. The element-wise analysis of assurance highlights that public sector banks in comparison to private sector banks show better performance as far as feeling safe with transacting the bank is concerned. The position of foreign banks on this element is quite satisfactory as is evident from the low negative SERVQUAL scores (-0.02 and -0.04). Public sector banks are again low as far as consistent courteous employees are concerned in comparison to foreign banks. The position of JKB on this element of assurance is in between the two extremes.

TABLE 4.4

Comparative SERVQUAL Scores of Banks on Assurance

Elements of Service Quality (Assurance)	*BANKS*				
	SBI	*PNB*	*JKB*	*CB*	*SCGB*
14. Employees who are trustworthy	-1.62	-1.59	-1.61	-0.74	-0.32
15. Feeling safe in transacting with the bank	-0.31	-0.39	-0.50	-0.02	-0.04
16. Employees who are consistently courteous	-1.83	-1.79	-1.39	-1.09	-0.35
17. Employees who have the knowledge to answer customers questions	-1.55	-1.60	-1.28	-1.34	-0.70
Assurance	-5.31	-5.37	-4.78	-3.19	-1.4
Rank	**4**	**5**	**3**	**2**	**1**

The element-wise analysis of assurance reveals that all Indian banks do not have consistent courteous employees. Indian banks also score low as far as trustworthy of employees and employees who have the knowledge to answer questions are concerned. This research finding is in line with the findings of Svinastava (1994). He reported that approximately 50% of the customers feel that bank employees are formal and casual in their approach while dealing with customers. However, the findings of Bhattacharya and Ghose (1989) are not in agreement with the above findings. They reported that about eighty four per cent respondents feel that banks have courteous employees. Lewis (1991) reported that honesty and trustworthiness are highly rated personal qualities among the US bank employees. This follows that courteous, trustworthyness, and knowledge of employees to answer customers questions play a significant role in determining the quality of service of banks, wherein our banks are deficient. This fact has also been brought to light by Sundaram (1984) and Gurdeep (1994) who hold the view that present customer service systems lack motivation and initiative, adversely affect the services offered, the process delaying the service and the poor motivation desensitizing the service. Banks have almost become bureaucratic organisation. Such statements lead us to conclude that banks do not have good working conditions as has also been revealed by Srivastava (1994).

Empathy

The data in Table 4.5 reveals that SCGB with low negative SERVQUAL score of -2.96 followed by CB -5.53 figures high on empathy dimension while as Indian banks with high negative SERVQUAL score -9.22, -9.06 and -8.00 are comparatively low on the said dimension.

The element-wise analysis of empathy reveals that Indian banks score too low on SERVQUAL as far as convenient operating hours are concerned. In other words data suggests poor services of Indian bank on this element in comparison to foreign banks. CB, however, figures low as far as the customer interest is concerned as is evident from low SERVQUAL score (-2.28). Again, all Indian banks figure low as far as banks that give personal attention are concerned in comparison to foreign banks.

TABLE 4.5

Comparative SERVQUAL Scores of Banks on Empathy

Elements of Service Quality (Assurance)	*BANKS*				
	SBI	*PNB*	*JKB*	*CB*	*SCGB*
18. Bank that gives individual attention	-1.55	-1.51	-1.48	-0.57	-0.38
19. Convenient operating hours	-2.09	-2.27	-1.93	-0.08	-0.12
20. Employees who give personal attention	-1.68	-1.58	-1.45	-0.77	-0.37
21. Bank which has your best interests at heart	-1.80	-1.88	-1.56	-2.28	-1.21
22. Employees who understand specific needs of the customer	-1.94	-1.98	-1.58	-1.83	-0.88
Empathy	-9.06	-9.22	-8.00	-5.53	-2.96
Rank	**04**	**05**	**03**	**02**	**01**

The SERVQUAL scores of Indian banks on empathy is too low compared to foreign banks. The position of CB is also not satisfactory on this dimension. Indian banks figure too low on three elements of empathy, viz., convenient operating hours, employees providing individualized attention, and bank that gives individual attention. The weak position of Indian banks on these elements of empathy suggests heavy investment in banking technology, which will definitely take care of these elements of empathy. Lakshmi (1991) highlighted this fact, in an empirical study, where 70% of the respondents opined that the present business timing of most banks was not at all convenient. Foreign banks figure high one these elements of empathy because of their technological edge. As already mentioned, public sector banks, in India are operating in all segments, in particular government transactions, which increase their work-load and in absence of large number of ATMs', banks continuously have to face music from their customers regarding operational hours and individual attention.

Overall Service Quality

To measure the overall service quality of banks, under study, mean scores on all dimensions of service quality were computed and are presented in Table 4.6. It is evident from Table 4.6 that SCGB figures highest on SERVQUAL score followed by CB, while as SBI stands low on SERVQUAL score. JKB and PNB ranked 3rd and 4th respectively on the said score. The table also highlights greater variation across all dimensions of service quality in the sample organisation. For example, SBI followed by PNB figures too low on tangibility (-2.40 and -2.12) while as CB (-0.16) followed by SCGB (-0.35) figure highest on said dimension. JKB ranked 3rd on tangibility. Both foreign banks as well as Indian banks are low on empathy and assurance dimension as indicated by the aforementioned data.

TABLE 4.6

Overall comparative SERVQUAL scores of banks averaged on all Dimensions

Service Quality Dimension	*BANKS*				
	SBI	*PNB*	*JKB*	*CB*	*SCGB*
Tangibility	-2.40	-2.12	-1.73	-0.16	-0.35
Reliability	-1.05	-0.96	-1.34	-0.33	-0.20
Responsiveness	-1.92	-1.77	-1.70	-0.61	-0.36
Assurance	-1.33	-1.34	-1.19	-0.79	-0.33
Empathy	-1.82	-1.84	-1.60	-1.10	-0.63
Total	-8.52	-8.03	-7.56	-2.99	-1.87
Rank	**5**	**4**	**3**	**2**	**1**

Unlike western countries, the nature and frequency of

studies in India concerning service quality/customer service in banks are extremely limited. These limited studies of academicians and practitioners have reported very poor service quality mostly in public sector banks (Brahmanandam and Narayana, 1990; Elias, 1982; Nageshwar and Promod, 1990; Nageswar, 1987; Nandakumar, 1995; Sesha Sai, 1999; Sundaram, 1984). The present study confirms such findings. However, it brings to light that poor service quality among Indian banks is mostly because of deficiency in tangibility and responsiveness. Public sector banks meet nearly 90% banking needs of the country (Basu, 1995) while other financial institutions meet the remaining10 percent. Retail banking constitutes eighty percent of their total banking business. Investment in relevant banking technology particularly ATM's and internet facility will take care of most of their retail banking and help in reducing customer grievances. This fact was realized much earlier when Rangararjan Committee Report (1989) stressed mechanization of Indian banks. Many other researchers have suggested banking technology as a means to improve customer services (Ammyya, 1996; Middleton, 1994; Saraf, 1997).

Importance of Service Quality Dimensions: A Comparison

To measure the importance of service quality dimensions, frequency tables were prepared. A weight of five was given to most important service quality dimension and a weight of one was given to least important service quality dimension. The results obtained from this analysis are presented in table 4.7.

Table 4.7 clearly reveals that the reliability is the most important service quality dimension for banks as well as for bank customers. This research finding is in line with the research findings of Lewis (1991) and Parasuraman (1985). Responsiveness, tangibility empathy and assurance emerged

2nd, 3rd, 4th and least important service quality dimension respectively except for SBI where assurance is the 4th important dimension and empathy the least important. It is also clear that customers of all the five banks do not exhibit greater variation as for as importance to service quality dimensions are concerned. Banks also show the same importance to service quality dimensions except JKB which shows empathy as the least important dimension. The table clearly depicts that banks meet the expectations of their customers as for as importance to service quality dimensions are concerned.

TABLE 4.7

Comparative Analysis of Importance of Service Quality Dimensions among Bank Officers and Bank Customers.

Service Quality Dimensions	*SBI*		*PNB*		*JKB*		*CB*		*SCGB*	
	BO	*BC*	*BO*	*BC*	*BO*	*BC*	*BO*	*BC*	*BO*	*BC*
Tangibility	2.91	3.10	3.28	3.18	2.79	2.55	2.72	3.04	2.87	2.81
Reliability	4.30	4.23	4.50	4.27	4.07	4.43	4.62	4.57	4.64	4.7
Responsiveness	3.89	4.20	3.55	4.19	3.88	3.88	4.24	4.39	3.62	4.08
Assurance	1.90	1.81	1.78	1.56	2.35	1.83	1.55	1.01	1.74	1.47
Empathy	2.00	1.67	1.88	1.83	1.91	2.00	2.34	2.00	2.13	1.92

Note: BO denotes bank officials and BC denotes bank customers

Table 4.7 reports the responses of bank officials and bank customers regarding importance to service quality dimensions and brings to light that reliability followed by responsiveness is the most important service quality dimension for both bank officials and bank customers. This finding is in line with the research findings of Parasuraman et al. (1988 and 1991), Lewis (1991) and Hart (1988). Tangibility emerged third important service quality dimension as reported by both bank officials and bank customers. However, Berry et al. (1994) reported tangibility as least important service quality dimension. Assurance followed by empathy is the least important service quality dimensions. The reverse was the findings of Berry et al. (1994). There exists little difference in the perceptions of bank officials and banks customers of SBI and JKB as far as importance to assurance and empathy is concerned. The findings lead us to conclude that bank officials have correct assessment as far as the perceptions of their customers regarding importance to service quality dimensions are concerned. But in India, there is no research evidence to support the present findings.

Service Quality Variation Across Demographic Variables

Service organisations need to provide consistent service quality to maintain/increase their market share/profitability. In an attempt to study whether banks, under study, provide same service quality to all their customers, respondents were divided into different groups based on demographic variables. Mean expectations and mean perceptions were calculated for different variables for each bank separately. SERVQUAL scores, accordingly, for different groups and for each bank were computed which are presented below.

Service Quality Variation and Income

With a view to measure the service quality by different income groups of sample organisation, respondents were grouped into four income groups, viz. Group 1st income up to Rs.15,000 p.m., group 2nd income Rs.15,000 – 25,000 p.m., group 3rd income between Rs.25,000 – 35,000 p.m. and group 4th where income exceeds Rs.35,000 per month. The comparative SERVQUAL scores are reported in Table 4.8. From the analysis of data, it is evident that SERVQUAL scores of SCGB followed by CB is comparatively high for all income groups whereas the SERVQUAL scores of SBI followed by PNB are comparatively low as reported by 1st and 2nd income groups respectively. The PNB's SERVQUAL score ranked 3rd as reported by 3rd income group while as the Bank scores comparatively low for higher income group. The J&K Bank's SERVQUAL score ranked 3rd and 4th, i.e., the Bank's service quality is in between the two nationalised and two foreign banks.

The dimension wise analysis shows serious shortfall for responsiveness for SBI followed by PNB and JKB as reported by 1st and 2nd income groups. This dimension (responsiveness), however, ranked 3rd for high-income groups except for PNB where it ranked 2nd on said dimension as has been reported by 3rd income group. The SERVQUAL scores of Indian banks figures high on reliability dimension as reported by all income groups except for JKB where income groups 4th ranked this dimension 2nd. For higher income groups, all Indian banks figure low on tangibility followed by empathy. Expectedly, foreign banks score high on tangibility dimension. However, the income groups of 2nd and 4th have ranked SCGB 4th on tangibility. A close examination of table 4.8 reveals that Indian banks figure low on responsiveness followed by tangibility whereas they figure high on reliability followed by assurance as reported by 1st and 2nd income groups. However, tangibility followed by empathy figures low whereas reliability followed by assurance figures high as reported by higher income groups.

From the analysis of table 4.8, it is clear that service quality of Indian banks as perceived by their customers increases as the level of income goes up. However, it is not necessary that there will be a proportionate increase in the quality of service delivered by Indian banks in relation to their level of income. This is because the higher income groups usually tend to be better educated, are aware about banking business and know their rights as bank customers. Contrary to high income groups, lower income groups usually are pension holders, who prefer to spend more time in branches to chat with their colleagues and front line staff, small money savers who are less educated, unaware of banking business and do not know their rights as bank customers.

Secondly, the number of low/medium income groups is considerably high compared to higher income groups. Foreign bank's service quality as perceived by respective respondents shows minor variation for one simple reason. These banks are very much selective in choosing a customer and their operation is in selected markets only. Besides these banks operate mostly through ATMs, which cannot recognize any difference in levels of income.

Service Quality Variation and Age

With a view to measure service quality variation, if any, of different age groups of sample organisation, respondents were categorised into three groups viz., 20 – 35; 35 – 50 and above 50. SERVQUAL scores were obtained for each group and for each bank separately which are presented in table 4.9. From the analysis of data in Table 4.9, it is evident that SCGB figures high on SERVQUAL scores across all dimensions followed by CB except in the 3rd age group where it is ranked 2nd. The SBI followed by PNB figures lowest on SERVQUAL score among all the three age groups. JKB, however, is in between the two extremes.

The dimension-wise analysis of table 4.9 reveals that in the age group of 20 – 35, both public sector banks figure high on SERVQUAL score on reliability followed by assurance while as they figure low on tangibility followed by responsiveness except for PNB which is ranked 3rd on responsiveness by the said age group. JKB scores high on assurance followed by reliability while as it scores low on responsiveness followed by tangibility. Foreign banks score low on empathy followed by assurance except for SCGB which ranked 1st on assurance. CB figures high on tangibility followed by reliability.

In the 2nd age group, all Indian banks figure low on tangibility followed by responsiveness except PNB which ranked 3rd on said dimension. Public sector banks scored high on reliability followed by assurance while as JKB scored quite opposite to public sector banks on said dimension. CB again figured high on tangibility followed by reliability while as it scored low on empathy followed by assurance. SCGB, on the other hand, figures high on reliability followed by tangibility and assurance whereas it scores low on empathy.

In the age group of above 50 all Indian banks figure high on reliability followed by assurance while as they score low on tangibility followed by responsiveness except for JKB which ranked 3rd on responsiveness. CB again, scores high on tangibility followed by reliability whereas SCGB figures high on reliability followed by assurance. SCGB figures low on tangibility followed by empathy.

The analysis of Table 4.9 clearly reveals that service quality of Indian banks is high at higher age groups whereas reverse is the case at lower age groups. The variation in service quality to different age groups should have been accompanied by some other information such as income, level of education or profession, which could help in the explanation of such a variation. In the absence of such information, it is difficult to understand/comprehend such variation. It is true as far as foreign banks are concerned.

Service Quality Variation and Region

To measure service quality/variation of sample organisation in different regions the universe of study, i.e., Northern India was divided into three geographic locations/ regions, viz., region 1st which covers J&K State, region 2nd covers whole of Punjab and region 3rd includes part of Haryana and Delhi. With a view to have an in-depth analysis about the quality of service, the banks provide to their customers, the results of which are presented in table 4.10. From table 4.10, it is evident that in region 1st SCGB followed by J&KB figures high on SERVQUAL scores (– 2.76 and – 8.25) while as SBI followed by PNB figures low on SERVQUAL score (– 10.78 and – 8.48) respectively. The dimension wise analysis of Table 4.10 reveals that in region 1st the SBI and PNB's SERVQUAL score on tangibility (– 2.71 and – 2.53) followed by responsiveness (– 2.38 and – 1.74) figures low while as these banks figure high on assurance (– 1.70 and – 1.26) followed by reliability (– 1.95 and – 1.38) respectively. The JKB figures high on SERVQUAL score for assurance (– 1.39) followed by tangibility (– 1.59) while as the bank scores low on responsiveness (- 1.98) followed by empathy (- 1.67) respectively. SCGB figures high on reliability followed by responsiveness while as the banks SERVQUAL score ranked low for tangibility followed by empathy.

In region 2nd, the data reveals that SCGB's overall SERVQUAL score figures high (-1.08) while as PNB followed by SBI figures low (-8.03 and –7.65) respectively on SERVQUAL score. The JKB ranked 2nd (-4.73) on this score. The dimension wise analysis of table 4.10 reveals that all Indian banks figure low on tangibility followed by responsiveness while as these banks figure high relatively on reliability followed by assurance except for JKB and SCGB which figure 2nd on reliability dimension. The SCGB's SERVQUAL is high on assurance followed by reliability while as it figures low on empathy followed by responsiveness.

In region 3rd, the SERVQUAL score of SCGB followed by CB is high (- 1.96 and -3.00) while as SBI followed by PNB figures low (-8.5 and -7.6) as indicated by the aforementioned table. The JKB ranked 3rd (-6.73) on SERVQUAL score. The dimension wise analysis reveals that SBI, PNB and JKB figures high on reliability followed by assurance while as these banks are low on empathy followed by tangibility except PNB and

JKB which ranked 3rd and 5th for tangibility. Foreign banks, expectedly, score high on tangibility followed by reliability where as they score low on empathy followed by assurance. The SERVQUAL score of foreign banks ranked 3rd for responsiveness.

Table 4.10 highlights service quality scores of sample organisation in three different regions. The data clearly reveals that all banks have comparatively high service quality scores in region 3rd i.e. Delhi whereas service quality scores are low in region 1st (J&K State). The obvious reason, for such service quality variations in different regions is the level of banking competition. As the level of competition intensifies, the quality of service accordingly goes up. This is true as nothing except tough competition makes companies more honest. It is tough competition in which consumer gets a fair deal. But unfortunately no research evidence is available on banking services and the level of competition or variation in service quality in different regions to corroborate present findings.

Service Quality Variation and Profession

To study service quality variation by profession, the respondents were categorised into business and service class groups. The SERVQUAL scores of the two groups for each bank is presented in table 4.11. The table clearly reveals that all banks provide, expectedly, better service quality to group 1st in comparison to group 2nd though quality of service of each bank varies considerably. The overall analysis of the table 4.11 reveals that SCGB followed by CB figures high on SERVQUAL score for both groups while as SBI followed by PNB and JKB figures low for both groups on SERVQUAL score.

The dimension wise analysis of group 1st reveals serious shortfall for tangibility followed by empathy for all Indian banks while as SERVQUAL scores on reliability is comparatively better. The SERVQUAL scores of foreign banks on all dimensions except empathy indicates high service quality standards.

The respondents of Indian banks, of group 2nd, have different perceptions about service quality dimensions. All Indian banks figure low on SERVQUAL score for responsiveness followed by empathy dimension except SBI, which ranked low on empathy followed by responsiveness. Group 1st (Business group) being familiar with banking business do not face many problems while dealing with their respective banks, compared to group 2nd. Also group 1st has comparatively large business with other banks and as a result receive comparatively better service quality from their respective banks.

Table 4.11 presents service quality scores as reported by business and service group respondents of all the banks. The data clearly reveals that all banks provide relatively better service quality to business group as compared to service group. The only reason for better service quality to group 1st is that their levels of income, is relatively, higher in comparison to group 2nd. This finding supports the earlier findings, which are reported in table 4.8.

Service Quality Variation and Level of Education

With a view to study service quality variation, if any, of sample organisation, at different levels of education, respondents were grouped into four education levels viz., level 1st Graduation/Diploma degree; level 2nd post-graduation/diploma; level 3rd technical/ professional education; and level 4th included higher levels of education. Mean expectations and perception of respondents at different levels of education were calculated for each bank separately and their SERVQUAL scores were accordingly computed which are presented in table 4.12. The overall analysis of the table 4.12 reveals that SCGB followed by CB figures high on SERVQUAL scores among all education groups. However, there are significant variations of service quality among Indian banks as reported by respective bank customers. The low SERVQUAL score of PNB (-8.18) followed by SBI i.e., (-8.15) and JKB (-6.20) indicates poor quality services in comparison to foreign banks- SCGB (-1.34) followed by CB (-3.37) as reported by 1st education level. The dimension wise analysis shows serious shortfall tangibility for followed by responsiveness among Indian banks.

The respondents of level 2nd (education) have different perceptions of their respective banks on service quality. Here SBI figures low on SERVQUAL score (-8.95) followed by JKB (-8.32) and PNB (-7.95) whereas foreign banks have maintained their position. Tangibility followed by responsiveness continues low on SERVQUAL score among Indian banks.

It is disappointing that JKB figures comparatively too low on SERVQUAL score (-11.15) among all banks as reported by the respondents of 3rd level of education. The bank figures low (-2.65) on responsiveness followed by empathy (-2.47). For this group, the service quality of PNB (-6.68) is relatively better in comparison to SBI (-8.67) among Indian banks.

There were no respondents of level 4th for SBI and CB. The JKB again figures low on SERVQUAL scores (-8.89) followed by PNB (-7.91) while as SCGB figures highest (-1.22) on SERVQUAL score. The dimension wise analysis, as reported by level 4th, shows shortfall of tangibility followed by empathy for PNB while as JKB figures low on responsiveness followed by empathy.

Table 4.12 presents perceptions of service quality variations among different educational groups of all the banks. The data of the table reveals minor service quality variation in

TABLE 4.8

Comparative SERVQUAL Scores of Different Income Groups

Service Quality Dimensions	*Up to Rs.15,000*					*Rs.15,000 –25,000*					*Rs.25,000 – 35,000*					*Above Rs.35,000*				
	SBI (N=46)	*PNB (N=53)*	*JKB (N=78)*	*CB (N=17)*	*SCGB (N=16)*	*SBI (N=81)*	*PNB (N=49)*	*JKB (N=58)*	*CB (N=30)*	*SCGB (N=35)*	*SBI (N=35)*	*PNB (N=55)*	*JKB (N=31)*	*CB (N=27)*	*SCGB (N=28)*	*SBI (N=35)*	*PNB (N=44)*	*JKB (N=32)*	*CB (N=25)*	*SCGB (N=25)*
Tangibility	-2.42 (4)	-2.27 (3)	-1.60 (2)	-0.16 (1)	-0.01 (1)	-2.38 (4.5)	-2.31 (4)	-1.67 (2)	-0.11 (1)	-0.64 (4)	-2.36 (5)	-2.00 (5)	-1.93 (5)	-0.09 (1)	-0.16 (2)	-2.42 (5)	-1.90 (5)	-2.22 (5)	-0.19 (1)	-0.37 (4)
Reliability	-1.45 (1)	-1.35 (1)	-1.59 (1)	-0.32 (2)	-0.25 (3)	-1.31 (1)	-1.27 (1)	-1.69 (3)	-0.33 (2)	-0.21 (1)	-0.71 (1)	-0.85 (1)	-0.89 (1)	-0.38 (2)	-0.14 (1)	-0.25 (1)	-0.55 (1)	-0.47 (2)	-0.28 (2)	-0.15 (1)
Responsiveness	-2.62 (5)	-2.34 (5)	-2.05 (5)	-0.64 (3)	-0.27 (4)	-2.38 (4.5)	-2.36 (5)	-1.95 (5)	-0.64 (3)	-0.28 (2)	-1.30 (3)	-1.03 (2)	-1.39 (3)	-0.71 (3.5)	-0.34 (3)	-0.57 (3)	-1.04 (3)	-0.64 (3)	-0.47 (3)	-0.27 (2)
Assurance	-1.72 (2)	-1.69 (2)	-1.71 (3)	-1.22 (4)	-0.17 (2)	-1.66 (2)	-1.70 (2)	-1.86 (4)	-0.83 (4)	-0.38 (3)	-0.93 (2)	-1.16 (3)	-1.04 (2)	-0.71 (3.5)	-0.37 (4)	-0.43 (2)	-0.81 (2)	-0.41 (1)	-0.70 (4)	-0.32 (3)
Empathy	-2.17 (3)	-2.31 (4)	-1.78 (4)	-1.23 (5)	-0.33 (5)	-2.23 (3)	-2.29 (3)	-1.59 (1)	-1.12 (5)	-0.73 (5)	-1.49 (4)	-1.47 (4)	-1.47 (4)	-1.12 (5)	-0.63 (5)	-0.70 (4)	-1.25 (4)	-0.94 (4)	-0.98 (5)	-0.53 (5)
Total	-10.38	-9.96	-8.73	-3.57	-1.03	-9.96	-9.93	-8.76	-3.03	-2.24	-6.79	-6.51	-6.72	-3.01	-1.64	-4.37	-5.55	-4.68	-2.62	-1.64
Overall Rank	**5**	**4**	**3**	**2**	**1**	**5**	**4**	**3**	**2**	**1**	**5**	**3**	**4**	**2**	**1**	**3**	**5**	**4**	**2**	**1**

Note: Figures within parenthesis represent ranks to the respective Service Quality Dimensions.

TABLE 4.9

Comparative SERVQUAL Scores Of Different Age Groups

Service Quality Dimensions	*Age 20 – 35*					*Age 35 – 50*					*Age Above 50*				
	SBI (N=31)	*PNB (N=29)*	*JKB (N=58)*	*CB (N=19)*	*SCGB (N=20)*	*SBI (N=101)*	*PNB (N=107)*	*JKB (N=100)*	*CB (N=64)*	*SCGB (N=65)*	*SBI (N=65)*	*PNB (N=65)*	*JKB (N=41)*	*CB (N=16)*	*SCGB (N=19)*
Tangibility	-2.67 (5)	-2.38 (5)	-1.42 (4)	-0.14 (1)	-0.28 (4)	-2.30 (5)	-2.19 (5)	-1.79 (5)	-0.14 (1)	-0.27 (2.5)	-2.42 (5)	-1.88 (5)	-2.02 (5)	-0.26 (1)	-0.65 (5)
Reliability	-1.31 (1)	-1.11 (1)	-1.38 (2)	-0.27 (2)	-0.27 (3)	-1.15 (1)	-1.00 (1)	-1.46 (2)	-0.36 (2)	-0.15 (1)	-0.75 (1)	-0.81 (1)	-1.01 (1)	-0.28 (2)	-0.19 (1)
Responsiveness	-2.29 (4)	-1.92 (3)	-1.69 (5)	-0.67 (3)	-0.25 (2)	-1.92 (4)	-1.76 (3)	-1.77 (4)	-0.66 (3)	-0.30 (4)	-1.74 (4)	-1.71 (4)	-1.51 (3)	-0.34 (3)	-0.46 (3)
Assurance	-1.63 (2)	-1.71 (2)	-1.25 (1)	-0.88 (4)	-0.23 (1)	-1.36 (2)	-1.26 (2)	-1.20 (1)	-0.78 (4)	-0.27 (2.5)	-1.12 (2)	-1.29 (2)	-1.09 (2)	-0.70 (4)	-0.44 (2)
Empathy	-2.06 (3)	-2.33 (4)	-1.40 (3)	-1.20 (5)	-0.47 (5)	-1.83 (3)	-1.81 (4)	-1.69 (3)	-1.12 (5)	-0.56 (5)	-1.66 (3)	-1.67 (3)	-1.65 (4)	-0.92 (5)	-0.82 (4)
Total	-9.94	-9.45	-7.14	-3.16	-1.50	-8.56	-8.02	-7.91	-3.06	-1.55	-7.69	-7.36	-7.28	-2.50	-2.56
Overall Rank	**5**	**4**	**3**	**2**	**1**	**5**	**4**	**3**	**2**	**1**	**5**	**4**	**3**	**1**	**2**

Note: Figures within parenthesis represent ranks to the respective Service Quality Dimensions.

TABLE 4.10

Comparative SERVQUAL Scores of Different Regions

Service Quality Dimensions	*J&k Region State* 1^{s}				*Punjab Region* 2nd				*Delhi Region* 3rd				
	SBI (N=44)	*PNB (N=46)*	*JKB (N=145)*	*SCGB (N=18)*	*SBI (N=123)*	*PNB (N=128)*	*JKB (N=25)*	*SCGB (N=35)*	*SBI (N=30)*	*PNB (N=27)*	*JKB (N=29)*	*CB (N=99)*	*SCGB (N=51)*
Tangibility	-2.71 (5)	-2.53 (5)	-1.59 (2)	-1.50 (5)	-2.32 (5)	-2.05 (5)	-1.60 (5)	-0.21 (3)	-2.23 (4)	-1.75 (3)	-2.55 (5)	-0.16 (1)	-0.03 (1)
Reliability	-1.95 (2)	-1.38 (2)	-1.62 (3)	-0.16 (1)	-0.77 (1)	-0.95 (1)	-0.59 (2)	-0.20 (2)	-0.08 (1)	-0.63 (1)	-0.57 (1)	-0.33 (2)	-0.22 (2)
Responsiveness	-2.38 (4)	-1.74 (4)	-1.98 (5)	-0.22 (2)	-1.76 (4)	-1.75 (3)	-0.84 (4)	-0.25 (4)	-1.86 (3)	-1.90 (4)	-1.06 (3)	-0.62 (3)	-0.42 (3)
Assurance	-1.70 (1)	-1.26 (1)	-1.39 (1)	-0.29 (3)	-1.23 (2)	-1.41 (2)	-0.58 (1)	-0.12 (1)	-1.16 (2)	-1.14 (2)	-0.71 (2)	-0.78 (4)	-0.05 (4)
Empathy	-2.04 (3)	-1.57 (30	-1.67 (4)	-0.59 (4)	-1.57 (3)	-1.87 (4)	-0.76 (3)	-0.30 (5)	-2.43 (5)	-2.18 (5)	-1.84 (4)	-1.11 (5)	-0.79 (5)
Total	-10.78	-8.48	-8.25	-2.76	-7.65	-8.03	-4.37	-1.08	-8.50	-7.60	-6.73	-3.00	-1.96
Overall Rank	4	3	2	1	3	4	2	1	5	4	3	2	1

Note: Figures within parenthesis represent ranks to the respective Service Quality Dimensions.

TABLE 4.11

Comparative SERVQUAL Scores Of Different Professional Groups

Service Quality Dimensions	Business (Group 1st)					Service (Group 2nd)				
	SBI (N=86)	*PNB* (N=117)	*JKB* (N=93)	*CB* (N=60)	*SCGB* (N=55)	*SBI* (N=111)	*PNB* (N=84)	*JKB* (N=106)	*CB* (N=39)	*SCGB* (N=49)
Tangibility	-2.39 (5)	-2.05 (5)	-1.83 (5)	-0.15 (1)	-0.27 (3)	-2.40 (4)	-2.22 (3)	-1.66 (2)	-0.18 (1)	-0.44 (3)
Reliability	-0.83 (1)	-0.72 (1)	-0.95 (2)	-0.35 (2)	-0.25 (2)	-1.22 (1)	-1.26 (1)	-1.69 (3)	-0.28 (2)	-0.57 (4)
Responsiveness	-1.44 (4)	-1.38 (3)	-1.30 (3)	-0.59 (3)	-0.28 (4)	-2.29 (3)	-2.31 (5)	-2.04 (5)	-0.64 (3)	-0.36 (1)
Assurance	-1.02 (2)	-1.12 (2)	-0.87 (1)	-0.76 (4)	-0.24 (1)	-1.57 (2)	-1.64 (2)	-1.48 (1)	-0.83 (4)	-0.43 (2)
Empathy	1.29 (3)	-1.53 (4)	-1.40 (4)	-1.07 (5)	-0.55 (5)	-2.51 (5)	-2.27 (4)	-1.79 (4)	-1.17 (5)	-0.64 (5)
Total	-6.97	-6.80	-6.35	-2.92	-1.59	-9.99	-9.70	-8.66	-3.10	-2.44
Overall Rank	**5**	**4**	**3**	**2**	**1**	**5**	**4**	**3**	**2**	**1**

Note: Figures within parenthesis represent ranks to the respective Service Quality Dimensions.

TABLE 4.12

Comparative SERVQUAL Scores Of Different Educational Groups

Service Quality Dimensions	*Level 1st Graduation/Diploma*					*Level 2nd Post-graduation/Diploma*					*Level 3rd Professional/Technical*					*Level 4th Higher Education*		
	SBI (N=108)	*PNB (N=108)*	*JKB (N=95)*	*CB (N=19)*	*SCGB (N=29)*	*SBI (N=74)*	*PNB (N=77)*	*JKB (N=81)*	*CB (N=65)*	*SCGB (N=63)*	*SBI (N=15)*	*PNB (N=10)*	*JKB (N=17)*	*CB (N=15)*	*SCGB (N=08)*	*PNB (N=06)*	*JKB (N=06)*	*SCGB (N=04)*
Tangibility	-2.41	-2.20	-1.78	-0.14	-0.28	-2.36	-2.01	-1.68	-0.17	-0.44	-2.50	-2.20	-1.94	-0.16	-0.12	-2.04	-1.13	+0.25
	(5)	(5)	(5)	(1)	(4)	(5)	(5)	(3)	(1)	(4)	(5)	(5)	(2)	(1)	(3)	(5)	(1)	(1)
Reliability	-0.98	-0.98	-1.03	-0.39	-0.20	-1.15	-0.90	-1.57	-0.32	-0.20	-0.97	-0.72	-1.85	-0.30	-0.03	-0.86	-1.76	-0.20
	(1)	(1)	(2)	(2)	(1)	(1)	(1)	(2)	(2)	(1)	(1)	(1)	(1)	(2)	(1)	(1)	(2)	(3)
Responsive-	-1.79	-1.81	-1.25	-0.71	-0.23	-2.11	-1.76	-1.97	-0.59	-0.40	-1.88	-1.40	-2.67	-0.59	-0.09	-1.83	-2.21	-0.31
ness	(4)	(3)	(3.5)	(3)	(3)	(4)	(3)	(5)	(3)	(1.5)	(3)	(4)	(5)	(3)	(2)	(3)	(5)	(4)
Assurance	-1.26	-1.35	-0.89	-0.95	-0.22	-1.40	-1.38	-1.30	-0.78	-0.40	-1.43	-1.02	-2.22	-0.64	-0.34	-1.21	-1.79	-0.06
	(2)	(2)	(1)	(4)	(2)	(2)	(2)	(1)	(4)	(1.5)	(2)	(2)	(3)	(4)	(4)	(2)	(3)	(2)
Empathy	-1.71	-1.84	-1.25	-1.18	-0.41	-1.93	-1.90	-1.80	-1.14	-0.68	-1.89	-1.34	-2.47	-0.89	-0.45	-1.97	-2.00	-0.90
	(3)	(4)	(3.5)	(5)	(5)	(3)	(4)	(4)	(5)	(5)	(4)	(3)	(4)	(5)	(5)	(4)	(4)	(5)
Total	-8.15	-.8.18	-6.20	-3.37	-1.34	-8.95	-7.95	-8.32	-3.00	-2.12	-8.67	-6.68	-11.15	-2.58	-1.03	-7.91	-8.89	-1.22
Overall Rank	**4**	**5**	**3**	**2**	**1**	**5**	**3**	**4**	**2**	**1**	**4**	**3**	**5**	**2**	**1**	**2**	**3 1**	

Note: Figures within parenthesis represent ranks to the respective Service Quality Dimensions.

banks among different educational groups. In other words, the findings of this study lead us to conclude that banks do not recognize different levels of education/education as a factor in differentiating customer/markets like income or profession. But unfortunately this finding does not find any research support and therefore needs further investigation.

Importance to Service Quality Dimensions and Income

The rank orders to service quality dimensions as reported by respective bank customers (falling in various income groups) are presented in table 4.13. It is evident from table 4.13 that reliability followed by responsiveness is the 1st and 2nd important service quality dimension for all income groups and for all banks except for SBI, PNB and CB where responsiveness followed by reliability is the 1st and 2nd important dimension, respectively for the income group of 1st and 2nd. Tangibility is the 3rd important service quality dimension for all income groups, except for JKB where income group 2nd reported tangibility the least important dimension. Empathy followed by assurance is the 4th and 5th important service quality dimension for all income groups except for JKB, SCGB and SBI where the respondents in the income group of 1st, 2nd, 3rd and 4th respectively reported empathy as the 4th and assurance as the least important service quality dimension.

Importance to Service Quality Dimensions and Age

It is evident from the analysis of the Table 4.14 that tangibility is the 3rd important service quality dimension for all the bank customers and for all age groups. In the age group of 20 – 35, reliability and responsiveness is the 1st and 2nd important service quality dimension for the respondents of PNB, JKB and SCGB while as responsiveness and reliability is the 1st and 2nd important service quality dimension for the respondents of SBI and CB. Empathy followed by assurance is least important service quality dimension for the respondents of SBI and JKB while reverse is the case for PNB, CB and SCGB customers.

In the age group of 35 – 50, reliability followed by responsiveness is the 1st and 2nd important service quality dimension for the respondents of PNB, JKB and SCGB while as reverse is the case for SBI and CB. Assurance is the least important service quality dimension followed by empathy for all banks except SBI where quite reverse is the case.

In the age group of above 50, reliability followed by responsiveness is the 1st and 2nd important service quality dimension for the respondents of JKB and SCGB while as assurance followed by empathy is the least important service quality dimension for the respondents of all banks. Responsiveness however, is the first important service equality dimension followed by reliability for the respondents of both public sector banks.

Importance to Service Quality Dimensions and Region

The importance to service quality dimensions as reported by respective bank customers (grouped into three geographical locations/regions) are presented in table 4.15. The table clearly reveals that in region 1st responsiveness followed by reliability is the most important service quality dimension for SBI while as empathy followed by assurance is the least important dimension. Tangibility followed by responsiveness is the most important dimension for PNB while as empathy followed by assurance is the least important. The respondents of JKB and SCGB reported reliability followed by responsiveness most important dimensions while as empathy followed by tangibility is the least important dimensions except for SCGB respondents who reported assurance as least important followed by tangibility and empathy.

In region 2nd, respondents of all the banks reported reliability followed by responsiveness as the most important dimension, except for PNB, where responsiveness ranked 3rd important dimension. Assurance followed by empathy has been reported by respondents of all the banks, under study, as least important dimension, except for SCGB where respondents reported empathy followed by assurance as least important service quality dimension.

In region 3rd, respondents of JKB, CB and SCGB reported reliability as most important service quality dimension followed by responsiveness while as assurance followed by empathy is the least important service quality dimension. The respondents of SBI and PNB reported responsiveness followed by reliability as the most important service quality dimension while as assurance followed by empathy is the least important. Tangibility, as reported by respondents of all banks, is the 3rd important service quality dimension.

Importance to Service Quality Dimensions and Profession

The levels of importance to service quality dimensions as reported by the respondents (categorised into business and service class) of various banks, under study, are presented in table 4.16. From the analysis of table 4.16, it is clear that tangibility figures 3rd important service quality dimension for all banks and for both groups (1st and 2nd). For the respondents of group 1st, reliability is the most important dimension followed by responsiveness except for SBI, respondents reported responsiveness as most important and reliability 3rd important dimension. Assurance is the least important dimension for all banks followed by empathy, as reported by group 1st except for SBI and JKB where respondents reported empathy least important dimension followed by assurance.

The respondents of group 2nd of SBI, PNB and CB have reported responsiveness as the most important service quality dimension followed by reliability while as reverse is the case for SCGB and JKB. The respondents of group 2nd, reported assurance as least important dimension followed by empathy except for SBI and JKB empathy is the least important followed by assurance.

Importance to Service Quality Dimensions and Education

The importance's to service quality dimensions, as reported by the respective respondents, of sample organisation, are presented in table 4.17. The table clearly reveals that tangibility is the 3rd important service quality dimension for all respondents and for all banks except for PNB, JKB, CB and SCGB where respondents of level 1st, 3rd and 4th reported tangibility 1st, 2nd and least important dimension. Respondents of the level 1st of SCGB, CB and JKB reported reliability as most important service quality dimension followed by responsiveness whereas the respondents of PNB and SBI reported reliability 3rd and 2nd important dimension respectively. Empathy is the least important dimension for the respondents of SBI, JKB and SCGB followed by assurance whereas reverse is the case for PNB and CB.

The respondents of level 2nd of all banks reported reliability as the most important service quality dimension followed by responsiveness. Assurance as reported by the respondents of all banks is the least important service quality dimension followed by empathy. Except for the respondents of JKB empathy is the least important dimension followed by assurance.

The respondents of level 3rd of all banks except SBI reported reliability as the most important service quality dimension. Reliability figured 2nd important dimension for the respondents of SBI and responsiveness is the most important dimension.

Responsiveness, however, is the 2nd important dimension for the respondents of SCGB, CB and JKB whereas the respondent of PNB responsiveness is the 3rd important dimension. Assurance continues to be the least important dimension followed by the empathy and vice versa as reported by the respondents of PNB and JKB.

Reliability followed by responsiveness is the most important service quality dimension for all respondents (level 4th) except for the respondents of SCGB where responsiveness and tangibility are of equal importance. The respondents of PNB have reported assurance as the least important dimension followed by empathy whereas the respondents of JKB and SCGB have reported these two dimensions of equal importance.

Tables 4.13 – 4.17 present views of respondents, who vary on demographic variables, off all the banks under study. The tables clearly reveal that customers of all the banks, on average, consider reliability as the most important service quality dimension followed by responsiveness while as assurance followed by empathy is the least important service quality dimension. This research finding is in line with the findings of Parasuraman et al. (1988, 1991), Lewis Barbara (1991), Hart (1988). These researchers found reliability as the most important service quality dimension. However, Berry et al., (1994) along with Zeithaml et al., (1990), while supporting the findings of above mentioned researchers regarding most important (reliability) service quality dimension, found tangibility as the least important service quality dimension followed by empathy. Their findings reveal assurance as 3rd important service quality dimension. As already stated tangibility emerged 3rd important service quality dimension whereas assurance followed by empathy is the least important service quality dimension as far as the findings of present study are concerned.

TABLE 4.13

Comparative SERVQUAL Scores of Different Income Groups

Quality Dimensions	*Group 1st* Up to Rs. 15,00					*Group 2nd* Rs. 15,000-25,000					*Group 3rd* Rs. 25,000-35,000					*Group 4th* Above Rs. 35,000				
	SBI (N=46)	*PNB* (N=53)	*JKB* (N=78)	*CB* (N=17)	*SCGB* (N=16)	*SBI* (N=81)	*PNB* (N=49)	*JKB* (N=58)	*CB* (N=30)	*SCGB* (N=35)	*SBI* (N=35)	*PNB* (N=55)	*JKB* (N=31)	*CB* (N=27)	*SCGB* (N=28)	*SBI* (N=35)	*PNB* (N=44)	*JKB* (N=32)	*CB* (N=25)	*SCGB* (N=25)
Tangibility	2.57 (3)	3.06 (3)	2.62 (3)	2.94 (3)	3.00 (3)	3.32 (3)	2.98 (3)	2.19 (5)	3.00 (3)	2.80 (3)	3.34 (3)	3.49 (3)	2.58 (3)	3.04 (3)	3.00 (3)	3.09 (3)	3.16 (3)	3.00 (3)	3.12 (3)	2.72 (3)
Reliability	4.02 (2)	3.74 (2)	4.13 (1)	4.41 (2)	4.69 (1)	4.07 (1)	4.00 (2)	4.40 (1)	4.43 (2)	4.54 (1)	4.46 (1)	4.58 (1)	4.81 (1)	4.63 (1)	4.82 (1)	4.66 (1)	4.82 (1)	4.88 (1)	4.76 (1)	4.84 (1)
Responsiveness	4.41 (1)	4.55 (1)	3.88 (2)	4.59 (1)	4.00 ()2 (2)	3.90 (2)	4.57 (1)	3.98 (2)	4.57 (1)	4.11 (2)	4.11 (2)	3.75 (2)	3.74 (2)	4.33 (2)	4.11 (2)	4.14 (2)	3.89 (2)	3.81 (2)	4.12 (2)	4.04 (2)
Assurance	1.93 (5)	1.81 (5)	2.37 (4)	1.00 (5)	1.93 (4)	1.86 (4)	1.61 (5)	2.72 (4)	1.00 (5)	1.34 (5)	1.57 (4)	1.44 (5)	1.77 (5)	1.00 (5)	1.25 (5)	1.63 (4)	1.30 (5)	1.59 (5)	1.04 (5)	1.60 (5)
Empathy	2.07 (4)	1.85 (4)	2.00 (5)	2.06 (4)	1.38 (5)	1.59 (5)	1.84 (43)	2.81 (3)	2.00 (4)	2.20 (4)	1.51 (5)	1.75 (4)	2.10 (4)	2.00 (4)	2.00 (4)	1.49 (5)	1.77 (4)	1.72 (4)	1.96 (4)	1.80 (4)

Note: Figures within parenthesis represent ranks to the respective Service Quality Dimensions.

TABLE 4.14

Importance to Service Quality Dimension Of Different Age Groups

Service Quality Dimensions	*Age 20 – 35*					*Age 35 – 50*					*Age Above 50*				
	SBI (N=31)	*PNB (N=29)*	*JKB (N=58)*	*CB (N=19)*	*SCGB (N=20)*	*SBI (N=101)*	*PNB (N=107)*	*JKB (N=100)*	*CB (N=64)*	*SCGB (N=65)*	*SBI (N=65)*	*PNB (N=65)*	*JKB (N=41)*	*CB (N=16)*	*SCGB (N=19)*
Tangibility	3.32 (3)	2.97 (3)	2.59 (3)	3.47 (3)	2.20 (3)	3.34 (3)	3.26 (3)	2.44 (3)	3.01 (3)	2.87 (3)	2.65 (3)	3.13 (3)	2.75 (3)	3.18 (3)	2.84 (3)
Reliability	4.10 (2)	4.38 (1)	4.29 (1)	4.47 (2)	4.70 (1)	4.33 (2)	4.36 (1)	4.45 (1)	4.60 (2)	4.69 (1)	4.15 (2)	4.08 (2)	5.56 (1)	4.50 (1)	4.78 (1)
Responsiveness	4.26 (1)	4.34 (2)	3/69 (2)	4.53 (1)	4.10 (2)	4.11 (1)	4.07 (2)	3.99 (2)	5.93 (1)	4.04 (2)	4.32 (1)	4.30 (1)	3.87 (2)	4.31 (2)	4.15 (2)
Assurance	1.87 (4)	1.59 (5)	2.24 (4)	1.00 (5)	1.55 (5)	1.68 (4)	1.56 (5)	2.21 (5)	1.00 (5)	1.44 (5)	1.91 (5)	1.55 (5)	1.80 (5)	1.06 (5)	1.47 (5)
Empathy	1.45 (5)	1.72 (4)	2.19 (5)	2.05 (4)	2.05 (4)	1.54 (5)	1.74 (4)	1.61 (4)	2.00 (4)	2.40 (4)	1.97 (4)	1.92 (4)	1.97 (4)	1.93 (4)	1.73 (4)

Note: Figures within parenthesis represent ranks to the respective Service Quality Dimensions.

TABLE 4.15

Importance to Service Quality Dimension Of Different Regions

Service Quality Dimensions	*J&K State-Region Ist*				*Punjab- Region 2nd*				*Delhi- Region 3rd*				
	SBI (N=44)	*PNB (N=46)*	*JKB (N=145)*	*SCGB (N=18)*	*SBI (N=123)*	*PNB (N=128)*	*JKB (N=25)*	*SCGB (N=35)*	*SBI (N=35)*	*PNB (N=30)*	*JKB (N=29)*	*CB (N=99*	*SCGB (N=51)*
Tangibility	2.93 (3)	4.74 (1)	2.05 (4)	2.50 (3.5)	3.33 (3)	3.40 (2)	3.28 (3)	3.11 (3)	2.43 (3)	2.44 (3)	2.86 (3)	3.03 (3)	2.73 (3)
Reliability	3.82 (2)	4.20 (3)	4.33 (1)	4.56 (1)	4.36 (1)	4.29 (1)	4.60 (1)	4.80 (1)	4.30 (2)	4.30 (2)	4.79 (1)	4.57 (1)	4.71 (1)
Responsiveness	4.27 (1)	4.33 (2)	3.86 (2)	4.00 (2)	4.12 (2)	4.11 (3)	3.80 (2)	3.86 (2)	4.43 (1)	4.33 (1)	4.07 (2)	4.39 (2)	4.25 (2)
Assurance	2.36 (4)	2.17 (4)	2.46 (3)	1.44 (5)	1.67 (5)	1.34 (5)	1.32 (5)	1.94 (4)	1.43 (5)	1.56 (5)	1.21 (5)	1.01 (5)	1.16 (5)
Empathy	1.61 (5)	1.30 (5)	1.99 (5)	2.50 (3.5)	1.51 (4)	1.90 (4)	2.00 (4)	1.29 (5)	2.40 (4)	2.37 (4)	2.07 (4)	2.00 (4)	2.16 (4)

Note: Figures within parenthesis represent ranks to the respective Service Quality Dimensions.

TABLE 4.16

Importance to Service Quality Dimensions Of Different Professional Groups

Service Quality Dimensions	*Business Class (Group 1st)*					*Service (Group 2nd)*				
	SBI (N=86)	*PNB (N=117)*	*JKB (N=93)*	*CB (N=60)*	*SCGB (N=55)*	*SBI (N=111)*	*PNB (N=84)*	*JKB (N=106)*	*CB (N=39)*	*SCGB (N=49)*
Tangibility	3.13 (2)	3.19 (3)	2.61 (3)	2.52 (3)	2.82 (3)	3.09 (3)	3.17 (3)	2.62 (3)	3.05 (3)	2.82 (3)
Reliability	3.10 (3)	4.64 (1)	4.61 (1)	4.75 (1)	4.85 (1)	4.12 (2)	3.53 (2)	4.27 (1)	4.28 (2)	4.55 (1)
Responsiveness	4.05 (1)	3.94 (2)	3.99 (2)	2.55 (2)	3.94 (2)	4.32 (1)	4.50 (1)	3.78 (2)	4.67 (1)	4.22 (2)
Assurance	1.81 (4)	1.55 (5)	1.97 (4)	1.02 (5)	1.62 (5)	1.76 (4)	1.58 (5)	2.28 (4)	1.00 (5)	1.31 (5)
Empathy	1.63 (5)	1.68 (4)	1.82 (5)	2.00 (4)	1.76 (4)	1.46 (5)	1.96 (4)	2.17 (5)	2.00 (4)	2.10 (4)

Note: Figures within parenthesis represent ranks to the respective Service Quality Dimensions.

TABLE 4.17

Importance to Service Quality Dimensions Of Different Educational Levels

Service Quality Dimensions	*Graduation/Diploma Degree (Level I[st])*					*Post Graduation/Diploma (Level 2nd)*					*Professional/Technical (Level 3rd)*					*Higher Education (Level 4th)*		
	SBI (N=108)	*PNB* (N=108)	*JKB* (N=95)	*CB* (N=19)	*SCGB* (N=29)	*SBI* (N=74)	*PNB* (N=77)	*JKB* (N=81)	*CB* (N=65)	*SCGB* (N=63)	*SBI* (N=15)	*PNB* (N=10)	*JKB* (N=17)	*CB* (N=15)	*SCGB* (N=08)	*PNB* (N=06)	*JKB* (N=06)	*SCGB* (N=04)
Tangibility	3.05	4.67	2.68	2.95	2.93	3.16	3.17	2.48	3.03	2.69	3.27	3.30	2.29	2.93	3.00	2.83	2.00	-3.50
	(3)	(1)	(3)	(3)	(3)	(3)	(3)	(3)	(3)	(3)	(3)	(2)	(3)	(3)	(3)	(3)	(5)	(1.5)
Reliability	4.17	3.28	4.47	4.53	4.83	5.69	4.79	4.33	4.58	4.62	4.13	4.70	4.53	4.33	4.87	4.67	4.83	5.00
	(2)	(3)	(1)	(1)	(1)	(1)	(1)	(1)	(1)	(1)	(2)	(1)	(1)	(1)	(1)	(1)	(1)	(1)
Responsie-ness	4.22	4.22	3.90	4.47	3.90	4.17	4.18	3.87	4.38	4.19	4.20	3.00	2.35	4.27	4.12	4.00	3.83	3.50
	(1)	(2)	(2)	(2)	(2)	(2)	(2)	(2)	(2)	(2)	(1)	(3)	(2)	(2)	(2)	(2)	(2)	(1.5)
Assurance	1.89	1.61	2.05	1.00	1.79	1.57	1.51	2.19	1.00	1.38	2.13	1.50	2.29	1.13	1.00	1.50	2.17	1.50
	(4)	(5)	(4)	(5)	(4)	(4)	(4)	(4)	(5)	(5)	(5)	(4.5)	(4)	(5)	(5)	(5)	(3.5)	(4.5)
Empathy	1.67	1.77	1.88	2.05	1.55	1.77	1.87	2.11	2.00	2.11	2.00	1.50	2.11	2.33	2.00	2.00	2.17	1.50
	(5)	(4)	(5)	(4)	(5)	(4)	(4)	(5)	(4)	(4)	(4)	(4.5)	(5)	(4)	(4)	(4)	(3.5)	(4.5)

Note: Figures within parenthesis represent ranks to the respective Service Quality Dimensions.

5

Customer Expectations and Perceptions

This chapter, besides, discussing the empirical findings regarding customer expectations and perceptions in sample organizations, highlights perceptual differences between banks and respective bank customers regarding quality of service in banks.

Introduction

Previous researches on service quality support the notion that perceived service quality stems from customers' comparison of what they wish to receive from firms and what they perceive actual service performance to be – which are formed on the basis of previous experience with a company, its competitors, and marketing mix inputs (Gronroos, 1982; Lehtinen and Lehtinen, 1982; Parasuraman, et al., 1985, 1988; Sasser, et al., 1978). Expectations relate, typically, to the elements of marketing mix, which may be extended in the service sector to include "physical evidence", "process", and "people". (Bloom and Bitner 1981).

The "physical environment" will include facilitating goods and tangible clues, which may be essential or peripheral to the service being bought, and which impinge on expectations and perceptions of service quality. "Process" refers to service delivery systems. If there are poor, employees are blamed and consumers perceive poor service quality. "People" comprises those service personnel (both customer contact and back-room staff) who are integral to the production of a service and, although their degree of contact with customers will vary, all have a vital contribution in the delivery of quality service. Service quality, as such, is viewed as the degree and direction of discrepancy between consumer's perceptions and expectations (Parasuraman, et al., 1985, 1988).

Dimension-Wise Analysis

The second objective of the study was to examine the expectations and perceptions of bank customers and banks officials regarding the quality of service in banks under study. The main area of questioning and analysis concerned customer expectations and perceptions in relation to service quality dimensions: tangibility, reliability, responsiveness, assurance and empathy. Expectations and perceptions were measured on a seven point strongly disagree/strongly agree scale. Mean differences between customer expectations and customer perceptions were calculated separately for all the banks followed by a T. Test.

Tangibility

Significant differences are reported between service quality perceptions of the customers of foreign banks and the customers of Indian banks on tangibility (Table 5.1). Though J&K Bank's mean difference 6.93 (Expectation-perception) is slightly better as compared to nationalized banks. Expectedly foreign banks score high on tangibility. The element wise analysis of tangibility variables reveals that CB meets the expectations of their customers as far as communication material and neatness of employees are concerned. Further investment on there two elements of tangibility would mean waste of resources.

All Indian banks fall below the expectations of their

customers on all elements of tangibility, in particular physical facilities, followed by up-to-date equipment. Indian banks have to make a substantial investment in these two elements of tangibility to meet the expectations of their customers besides communication material and neatness of employees. The mean difference shows that Indian banks, SBI (9.59) followed by PNB (8.50) are below the expectations of their customers while as foreign banks CB (.66) followed by SCGB (1.39) are very close to the expectations of their customers as far as tangibility is concerned.

Reliability

As revealed by Table 5.2 there are significant differences in service quality perceptions of customers of foreign banks and Indian banks on reliability. Within foreign banks, the mean difference on reliability of SCGB is low (0.92) as compared to mean difference of CB customers (1.65), which shows that these banks also fall short of customer expectations. However, among Indian banks the mean difference on reliability of JKB (6.71) is high followed by SBI (5.23) and PNB (4.79), which indicates that these banks respectively fall much below their customer expectations.

Element wise analysis on reliability shows that SCGB followed by CB exceeds customer expectations on correct record keeping. However, these banks also fall slightly short of their customer expectations on remaining 4 elements of reliability as is evident from their mean differences. All Indian banks show a wide gap between customer expectations and perceptions on all elements of reliability dimension. In particular, in respect of delivering the service at promised time, the JKB falls much below the customer expectation (1.51 mean differences) followed by SBI (1.23) and PNB (1.13).

Responsiveness

Table 5.3 shows that again SCGB followed by CB figures

comparatively high on responsiveness, as their mean differences between customer expectations and perceptions are 1.29 and 2.45 respectively. Among Indian banks, SBI figures lowest on responsiveness as is evident from mean difference (7.69) followed by PNB (7.08) and JKB (6.80). Element wise analysis of responsiveness shows that in case of SBI mean difference ranged from 1.46 to 2.27 while as in case of PNB the mean difference ranged from 1.20 to 2.25. The mean difference of JKB between customer expectations and perceptions ranged from 1.43 to 1.95. The mean difference of foreign banks is low indicating quick response to customer services. To meet customer expectation of this level is certainly a major challenge, although there remain differences between customer expectations and perceptions.

Assurance

The study indicates that PNB with the mean difference of 5.37 falls below customer expectations as compared to SBI (5.31), JKB (4.79), CB (3.18) and SCGB (1.35) respectively (Table 5.4). The element wise analysis of assurance shows that, among foreign banks, CB followed by SCGB, exceed customer expectations as for as consistent courteous employees are concerned. The perception of customers of Indian banks in better as far as feeling safe in transacting with the bank is concerned because the mean difference between customer expectations and perceptions ranges from 0.31 to 0.50 only. But foreign banks (CB followed by SCGB) exceed the expectations of their respective customers on the said element of assurance.

Empathy

The data on Table 5.5 reveals that all but one of the elements of empathy, i.e., convenient operating hours records a high mean difference between customer expectation and perceptions of SBI (209) followed by PNB (2.27) and JKB

(1.93) indicating thereby that Indian banks are below the expectations of their customers. Foreign banks (CB followed by SCGB) having technology edge, score high on the said element. SBI falls much below the customer expectations comparatively on empathy as is evident from high mean difference (9.06) followed by JKB (8.01) and PNB (7.24). The mean difference of CB (5.53) in comparison to SCGB (2.95) shows a wide gap between customer expectations and perceptions.

Over all Analysis

The over-all analysis of table 5.6 reveals that SCGB followed by CB with low mean difference shows that foreign banks also fall short of their customer expectations. But the gap between customer expectations and perceptions is narrow when compared to Indian banks, i.e. their service quality is better in comparison to Indian banks. The SBI followed by PNB and JKB figure much below the customer expectations as reported by respective customers.

Consumers judge service quality relative to what they want. They view a firm's service quality by comparing their perceptions of service experiences with their expectations of what the service performance should be. A service quality gap results when service perceptions fall shor of their customers expectations.

A review of marketing literature reveals that, in India, little attention has been given to the consumer's evaluation process with regard to service quality and the limited studies available on the subject are mostly descriptive in nature. Two major reasons for this lake of empirical knowledge and explanatory analysis can be identified. First, quality has not been regarded as a first order variable in the management process among service firms. Second, since services are for the most part intangible, it is extremely difficult to

TABLE 5.1

Customer Expectations and Perceptions about Tangibility

Elements of Service Quality Dimension (Tangibility)	Group	SBI Mean	SBI STD. Dev.	SBI M.D.	SBI T. Value	PNB Mean	PNB STD. Dev.	PNB M.D.	PNB T. Value	JKB Mean	JKB STD. Dev.	JKB M.D.	JKB T. Value	CB Mean	CB STD. Dev.	CB M.D.	CB T. Value	SCGB Mean	SCGB STD. Dev.	SCGB M.D.	SCGB T. Value
1. Up-to-date equipment	E	6.74	0.46	2.64	36.28*	6.83	0.42	2.41	34.09*	6.51	0.89	1.75	15.37*	6.86	0.35	0.33	6.43*	6.75	0.48	0.45	4.10*
	P	4.10	0.89			4.42	0.91			4.76	1.36			6.53	0.50			6.30	1.24		
2. Physical Facilities	E	6.78	0.44	3.31	42.90*	6.83	0.41	2.83	33.78*	6.42	0.96	1.86	17.77*	6.89	0.32	0.31	5.51*	6.79	0.41	0.52	4.19*
	P	3.47	1.00			4.00	1.11			4.56	1.33			6.58	0.52			6.27	1.37		
3. Neatness of employees	E	6.97	0.22	1.79	34.44*	6.96	0.20	1.52	26.75*	6.60	0.78	1.61	16.14*	6.95	0.22	0.00	0.00	6.92	0.33	0.27	4.49*
	P	5.18	0.20			5.44	0.80			4.98	1.32			6.95	0.22			6.65	0.72		
4. Communication material	E	6.95	0.24	1.84	22.27*	6.94	0.28	1.74	24.92*	6.45	1.04	1.70	15.58*	6.90	0.30	0.01	0.22*	6.90	0.38	0.15	2.67*
	P	5.11	0.28			5.20	0.95			4.75	1.55			6.89	0.32			6.75	0.63		
Tangibility (01+02+03+04)	E	27.44	1.10	9.59	52.82*	27.55	1.00	8.50	41.63*	25,98	3.17	6.93	20.83*	27.60	0.74	0.66	5.62*	27.37	1.34	1.39	4.38*
	P	17.85	2.38			19.05	2.78			19.05	4.33			26.94	1.07			25.97	3.79		

E&P denotes customer expectations and perceptions respectively. *P<0.01; ** P< 0.05; *** P<0.10

Bank:	SBI	PNB	JKB	CB	SCGB
Number:	197	201	199	99	104
df:	196	200	198	98	103

TABLE 5.2

Customer Expectations and Perceptions about Reliability

Elements of Service Quality Dimension (Reliability)	Group	SBI Mean	SBI STD. Dev.	SBI M.D.	SBI T. Value	PNB Mean	PNB STD. Dev.	PNB M.D.	PNB T. Value	JKB Mean	JKB STD. Dev.	JKB M.D.	JKB T. Value	CB Mean	CB STD. Dev.	CB M.D.	CB T. Value	SCGB Mean	SCGB STD. Dev.	SCGB M.D.	SCGB T. Value
5. Promise to do something by a certain time, doing it	E	6.83	0.38	1.23	16.35*	6.73	0.46	1.13	20.44*	6.49	0.80	1.51	13.80*	6.75	0.44	0.33	4.71*	6.71	0.46	0.22	3.53*
	P	5.60	1.05			5.60	0.74			4.98	1.44			6.42	0.50			6.49	0.52		
6. Being sincere in solving the problem	E	6.82	0.41	1.19	14.74*	6.75	0.48	1.10	16.80*	6.51	0.96	1.42	11.26*	6.91	0.29	0.44	7.45*	6.87	0.40	0.55	4.04*
	P	5.63	1.15			5.65	0.89			5.09	1.57			6.46	0.52			6.65	0.55		
7. Performing the service right the first time	E	6.74	0.48	1.19	14.80*	6.69	0.47	1.09	17.69*	6.40	1.07	1.36	11.34*	6.80	0.40	0.23	3.54*	6.67	0.49	0.11	2.09*
	P	5.55	1.13			5.60	0.87			5.04	1.36			6.57	0.50			6.56	0.54		
8. Providing the service at the promised time	E	6.84	0.37	1.14	16.23*	6.79	0.45	1.08	17.59*	6.46	0.90	1.49	12.13*	6.82	0.39	0.69	12.95*	6.79	0.41	0.36	6.15*
	P	5.71	1.00			5.71	0.79			4.97	1.51			6.13	0.34			6.43	0.52		
9. Keeping records correctly	E	6.94	0.28	0.48	8.27*	6.96	0.21	0.40	9.81*	6.67	0.77	0.95	9.21	6.96	0.20	-0.03	-1.34	7.00	0.00	0.02	1.42
	P	6.46	0.92			6.56	0.56			5.72	1.58			6.99	0.10			6.98	0.02		
Reliability (5+6+7+8+9)	E	34.17	1.50	5.23	16.66*	33.91	1.63	4.79	21.14*	32.53	3.45	6.71	14.78*	34.23	1.13	1.65	11.52*	34.04	1.39	0.92	6.17*
	P	28.94	4.69			29.12	3.24			25.81	6.24			32.58	0.86			33.12	1.49		

Note: Refer to Table 5.1 for details related to E & P, level of significance, N and df .

TABLE 5.3

Customer Expectations and Perceptions about Responsiveness

Elements of Service Quality Dimension (Responsiveness)	Group	SBI Mean	SBI Dev.	SBI STD. M.D.	SBI T. Value	PNB Mean	PNB Dev.	PNB STD. M.D.	PNB T. Value	JKB Mean	JKB Dev.	JKB STD. M.D.	JKB T. Value	CB Mean	CB Dev.	CB STD. M.D.	CB T. Value	SCGB Mean	SCGB Dev.	SCGB STD. M.D.	SCGB T. Value
10. Telling customers exactly when services will be performed	E	6.85	0.36	1.46	20.03*	6.70	0.50	1.20	18.17*	6.41	0.96	1.43	12.97*	6.76	0.43	0.43	7.14*	6.76	0.43	0.30	5.47*
	P	5.39	1.01			5.50	0.87			4.98	1.41			6.33	0.52			6.46	0.52		
11. Employees providing prompt service to customers	E	6.88	0.32	2.23	21.55*	6.83	0.42	2.04	22.29*	6.69	0.64	1.95	15.70*	6.79	0.41	0.68	8.93*	6.80	0.40	0.28	4.40*
	P	4.65	1.42			4.79	1.33			4.74	1.72			6.11	0.68			6.52	0.70		
12. Employees who are always wiling to help	E	6.90	[illegible]	1.72	18.09*	6.82	0.43	1.60	19.47*	6.63	0.75	1.76	13.52*	6.86	0.35	0.53	6.87*	6.85	0.36	0.29	4.08*
	P	5.18	1.32			5.22	1.14			4.87	1.69			6.33	0.69			6.56	0.64		
13. Employees who are never too busy to respond to customers requests	E	6.79	0.56	2.27	21.09*	6.79	0.43	2.25	22.99*	6.31	1.25	1.66	12.31*	6.87	0.37	0.83	9.88*	6.78	0.42	0.42	6.23
	P	4.52	1.43			4.54	1.42			4.65	1.55			6.04	0.75			6.36	0.71		
Responsiveness (10+11+12+13)	E	27.43	1.18	7.69	23.07*	27.13	1.49	7.08	24.53*	26.04	3.02	6.80	15.77*	27.27	1.22	2.45	12.29*	27.18	1.24	1.29	6.82*
	P	19.74	4.66			20.05	4.22			19.24	5.73			24.82	1.73			25.89	2.04		

Note: Refer to Table 5.1 for details related to E & P, level of significance, N and df.

TABLE 5.4

Customer Expectations and Perceptions about Assurance

Elements of Service Quality Dimension (Assurance)	Group	SBI Mean	SBI STD. Dev.	SBI M.D.	SBI T. Value	PNB Mean	PNB STD. Dev.	PNB M.D.	PNB T. Value	JKB Mean	JKB STD. Dev.	JKB M.D.	JKB T. Value	CB Mean	CB STD. Dev.	CB M.D.	CB T. Value	SCGB Mean	SCGB STD. Dev.	SCGB M.D.	SCGB T. Value
14. Employees who are trustworthy	E	6.93	0.27	1.62	20.26*	6.91	0.29	1.59	22.02*	6.68	0.72	1.61	13.71*	6.89	0.32	0.74	11.31*	6.90	0.33	0.31	4.71*
	P	5.31	1.17			5.32	1.01			5.07	1.59			6.15	0.56			6.59	0.63		
15. Feeling safe in transacting with the bank	E	6.93	0.29	0.31	6.79*	6.92	0.28	0.40	7.88*	6.59	0.96	0.50	6.33*	6.97	0.17	-0.02	-1.00	6.93	0.29	-0.04	-1.07*
	P	6.62	0.66			6.52	0.70			6.09	1.36			6.99	0.10			6.97	0.22		
16. Employees who are conistently courteous	E	6.86	0.39	1.83	20.20*	6.84	0.37	1.79	22.74*	6.51	0.86	1.39	12.69*	6.87	0.34	1.09	16.16*	6.83	0.40	0.35	5.43*
	P	5.03	1.22			5.05	1.10			5.12	1.44			5.78	0.58			6.48	0.59		
17. Employees who have the knowledge to answer	E	6.79	0.43	1.55	18.02*	6.80	0.46	1.60	22.85*	6.48	0.92	1.28	13.24*	6.84	0.37	1.35	13.21*	6.79	0.43	0.70	7.13*
	P	5.24	1.14			5.20	0.99			5.20	1.40			5.49	0.90			6.09	0.93		
Assurance (14+15+16+17)	E	27.51	1.02	5.31	20.98*	27.46	1.12	5.37	24.09*	26.26	2.76	4.79	14.55*	27.57	0.83	3.16	18.26*	27.45	1.09	1.32	7.19*
	P	22.20	3.61			22.09	3.24			21.47	4.82			24.41	1.45			26.13	1.83		

Note: ***Refer to Table 5.1 for details related to E & P, level of significance, N and df .***

TABLE 5.5

Customer Expectations and Perceptions about Empathy

Elements of Service Quality Dimension (Empathy)	Group	SBI Mean	SBI STD. Dev.	SBI M.D.	SBI T. Value	PNB Mean	PNB STD. Dev.	PNB M.D.	PNB T. Value	JKB Mean	JKB STD. Dev.	JKB M.D.	JKB T. Value	CB Mean	CB STD. Dev.	CB M.D.	CB T. Value	SCGB Mean	SCGB STD. Dev.	SCGB M.D.	SCGB T. Value
18. Bank that give individual attention	E	6.84	0.41	1.56	18.97*	6.84	0.41	1.52	19.73*	6.41	1.10	1.49	12.28*	6.86	0.35	0.57	8.36*	6.81	0.42	0.39	5.70*
	P	5.28	1.19			5.32	1.05			4.29	1.65			6.29	0.56			6.42	0.63		
19. Convenient operating hours	E	6.94	0.26	2.09	19.16*	6.93	0.30	2.27	21.84*	6.48	1.00	1.93	14.74*	6.96	0.20	0.08	2.03**	6.95	0.26	0.11	2.03**
	P	4.85	1.57			4.66	1.43			4.55	1.67			6.88	0.33			6.84	0.66		
20. Employees who give personal attention	E	6.85	0.44	1.68	18.66*	6.77	0,45	1.58	20.20*	6.32	1.19	1.46	11.22*	6.83	0.38	0.77	12.66*	6.77	0.45	0.37	5.14*
	P	5.17	1.24			5.19	1.07			4.86	1.65			6.06	0.45			6.40	0.73		
21. Bank which has your best interests at least	E	6.79	0.50	1.80	20.18*	6.77	0.47	1.88	22.40*	6.29	1.10	1.56	13.49*	6.92	0.27	2.28	20.69*	6.94	0.27	1.21	11.57*
	P	4.99	1.17			4.89	1.13			4.73	1.55			4.64	1.07			5.73	1.13		
22. Employees who under-stand specific needs of the customers	E	6.78	0.50	1.94	20.38*	6.73	0.57	1.98	24.61*	6.39	0.83	1.58	15.11*	6.98	0.14	1.83	22.49*	6.91	0.32	0.87	9.57*
	P	4.84	1.28			4.75	1.14			4.81	1.52			5.15	0.77			6.04	0.90		
Empathy (18+19+20+21+22)	E	34.19	1.72	9.06	23.43*	34.02	1.87	7.24	23.93*	31.88	4.32	8.01	16.09*	34.55	0.88	5.53	20.78*	34.38	1.27	2.95	9.43*
	P	25.13	4.44			26.78	4.28			23.87	5.94			29.02	1.48			31.43	2.58		

Note: Refer to Table 5.1 for details related to E & P, level of significance, N and df.

TABLE 5.6

Customer Expectations and Perceptions about Overall Service Quality in Banks

		BANKS																			
Overall Service Quality		*SBI*				*PNB*				*JKB*				*CB*				*SCGB*			
	Group	*Mean*	*STD. Dev.*	*M.D.*	*T. Value*	*Mean*	*STD. Dev.*	*M.D.*	*T. Value*	*Mean*	*STD. Dev.*	*M.D.*	*T. Value*	*Mean*	*STD. Dev.*	*M.D.*	*T. Value*	*Mean*	*STD. Dev.*	*M.D.*	*T. Value*
Overall	E	150.75	5.17			150.07	5.57			142.69	14.40			151.21	4.07			150.42	4.98		
Service				34.95	30.65*			32.98	31.80*			31.65	20.36*			11.61	20.17*			7.01	9.14*
Quality	P	115.80	16.77			117.09	15.24			111.04	22.79			139.60	3.92			143.41	9.42		

Note: Refer to Table 5.1 for details related to E & P, level of significance, N and df.

conceptualize and measure quality (Bateson, 1977; Berry 1980; Gronroos, 1978; Lovelock, 1981). Tables 5.1-5.6 depict customer expectations and perceptions regarding service quality of each bank under study. All these tables reveals high mean differences in Indian banks compared to foreign banks, which indicates that Indian banks are much below the expectations of their customers in comparison to foreign banks. These results find evidence in the Goiporia Committee Report (Sesha Sai, 1999), which noted, "notwithstanding the rationale that is given for the deficiencies in customers' service, an important fact that cannot be overlooked, is that, the society in general is expecting much more from the banks that they are able to give at present. While looking at the causes for customer complaints, it is imperative for us to analyse as to why in spite of so many measures taken for improvement of customer service, the level of satisfaction as perceived by many sections of the society is low". Some eighty of the Committees ninety-seven recommendations have since been operationlised by banks and are being followed up and reviewed. This observation undoubtedly reveals that Indian banks do not meet the expectations of their customers. Many scholars (Mankidy, 2000; Muniraj, 1994; Nageswar and Pramod, 1990; Ramachandra, 1992; Sundaram, 1984); and Practitioners (Middleton, 1994; Saraf, 1997; Srinivas, 1996) have similar observations regarding the quality of service, about Indian public sector banks. Though there is no empirical evidence to support such findings. This state of affairs leads us to conclude that customer expectations, in India, have increased considerably particularly after liberalization in 1991. Foreign banks and non-bank institutions, which are backed by banking technology, have raised the aspirations of the customers of other banks. In delivery of service, it is speed, accuracy, promptness, reliability etc. which matters and which can be ensured through relevant technology backup wherein our banks are lagging behind. This I feel is the contributing factor as far as high mean differences in Indian banks are concerned. Foreign banks, in comparison to Indian banks, are much nearer to the expectations of their customer. These banks, unlike Indian banks operate in selected segments and mostly through ATM's and internet and have more time to attend to customers resulting in high level of customer satisfaction.

Service Quality Perceptions: A Comparison

Related to the 2nd objective of the study was to assess the perceptions of bank officials and their respective customers about the quality of services. To achieve this objective, perceptions were measured on a seven-point (strongly disagree/strongly agree) scale. Mean perceptions of individual banks and their respective customers were computed followed by a T. Test. The results obtained from this computation are presented in Tables 5.7-5.12.

Tangibility

The analsyis of Table 5.7 reveals high differences between the perceptions of foreign banks/officials and their respective customers on tangibility and the perceptions of Indian banks and their respective customers on this dimension. The data on tangibility reveals that foreign banks (CB followed by SCGB) with low mean difference of –1.13 and –0.90 respectively exceed the perceptions of their customers while as Indian banks with high mean difference, particularly SBI (5.28) followed by JKB (4.25) and PNB (4.16), fall much below the perceptions of their customers on this dimensions. The element wise analysis of tangibility shows serious shortfall of perceptions among Indian banks on up-to-date equipments and physical facilities available in a bank in comparison to the perceptions of their respective customers.

Reliability

As is evident from the data on reliability dimension there exists a wide gap between the perceptions of Indian banks and the perceptions of their respective customers (Table 5.8). The JKB's high mean difference (5.55) followed by SBI (3.37) and PNB (2.58) shows the level of incorrect assessment of perceptions as compared to the perceptions of their respective customers. Foreign banks are exceeding the perceptions of their customers on this dimension. The element wise analysis of reliability shows that Indian banks fall short of correct assessment on respective consumer perceptions as far as keeping the promise and being sincere in solving the problems are concerned.

Responsiveness

The data on responsiveness (Table 5.9) shows that there is little difference between the perceptions of foreign banks and their respective customers. Indian banks, particularly JKB followed by SBI's perceptual difference is wide on responsiveness. JKB followed by SBI with high mean difference of 5.01 and 3.64 shows that there exists a wide gap between the perceptions of these banks and their respective customers. The element-wise analysis shows that Indian banks are falling below the perceptions of their respective customers as far as employees providing prompt services are concerned.

Assurance

The perceptual difference between officers of JKB and its customers on service quality (assurance dimension) is high as is evident from the mean difference (3.9) in table 5.10. The respondents of SBI and PNB have also given low rating on assurance dimension to their respective banks compared to the ratings of respective banks. It is clear that Indian bank fall below the perceptions of their respective customers. Contrary to Indian banks, the perceptual difference, on assurance, between foreign banks and their respective customers is comparatively low. The element-wise analysis of assurance shows that SCGB followed by CB are exceeding the perceptions of their customers as far as trustworthiness of employees and employees providing prompt services are concerned.

Empathy

Table 5.11 reveals that Indian banks stand for away from their customers as far as perception on this dimension are concerned. There exists a wide gap between the perception of banks (especially JKB followed by PNB and SBI) and their respective customers as is evident from high mean differences (7.46, 6.05 and 5.50 respectively). However, it is surprising to note that even CB is falling below the perceptions of their customers (4.09) on this dimension. The element-wise analysis shows that foreign banks (CB followed by SCGB) are exceeding the perceptions of their customers as far as banks individualized attention and convenient operating hours are concerned.

Overall Perceptual Difference

The overall analysis of Table 5.12 reveals that there exists a wide perceptual difference on service quality among Indian banks and their customers whereas the perceptual difference on service quality between foreign banks and their customers is narrow. The high mean difference of JKB (25.36) followed by SBI (20.68) and PNB (18.17) shows that these banks have incorrect assessment about the quality of service they are delivering to their respective customers. A low mean difference of SCGB (1.67) followed by CB (4.91) shows that there is negligible perceptual difference between foreign banks and their respective customers about the quality of service.

In India there is no research evidence regarding perceptual differences in service quality between bank officers and bank customers. The present study, of course, is aimed to fill up this research gap. Table 5.7 reveals that foreign banks are exceeding the perceptions of their customers on tangibility in comparison to Indian banks. This follows that Indian banks, particularly SBI followed by JKB have incorrect assessment about the quality of services they are delivering to their respective customers. J&K is much below the expectations of their customers on reliability as in evident from high mean difference in comparison to other banks. Banking competition is almost absent in JKB state because of political disturbance. As a result, JKB has a monopoly in banking business in J&K state. Monopoly firms/service providers always have a wrong notion of being the best firms/service providers. Because of this wrong notion they (JKB) have incorrect assessment about the quality of service they are delivering to their customers. Overall it is not a good sign that all Indian banks, especially JKB followed by SBI and PNB do not have correct assessment about the quality of service they are delivering to their customers.

To sum up, the results of this chapter lead us to conclusion that foreign banks are exceeding the expectations of their customers while as Indian banks are much below the expectations of their customers. The perceptual difference regarding service quality is low between foreign banks and their customers where as the said difference is high among Indian banks and their customers. This follows that Indian banks besides having incorrect assesement about customer expectations and perceptions also have a wrong notion about the quality of service they are delivering to their customers. With a view to identify variation in specific service quality dimension/s, an attempt has been made in the next chapter to analyse variation in service quality among the sample organizations. This chapter also makes a comparative analysis of service quality among the banks under reference.

TABLE 5.7

Comparative Perceptions of Bank Officers and Customers about Tangibility

Elements of Service Quality Dimension (Tangibility) Value	*Group*	*SBI Mean*	*SBI STD. Dev.*	*SBI M.D.*	*SBI T. Value*	*PNB Mean*	*PNB STD. Dev.*	*PNB M.D.*	*PNB T. Value*	*JKB Mean*	*JKB STD. Dev.*	*JKB M.D.*	*JKB T. Value*	*CB Mean*	*CB STD. Dev.*	*CB M.D.*	*CB T. Value*	*SCGB Mean*	*SCGB STD. Dev.*	*SCGB M.D.*	*SCGB T. Value*
1. Up-to-date equipment	BO	5.63	0.68	1.53	15.04***	5.39	1.01	0.97	8.38***	5.86	1.09	1.10	7.06***	6.24	0.51	-0.28	-2.66***	6.05	0.45	-0.25	-1.23
	BC	4.10	0.89			4.42	0.91			4.76	1.36			6.53	0.50			6.30	1.24		
2. Physical Facilities	BO	5.35	0.97	1.89	15.42***	5.56	0.90	1.57	12.20***	5.86	0.98	1.30	8.71***	6.28	0.53	-0.30	-2.73***	6.05	0.68	-0.22	-0.9
	BC	3.47	1.00			4.00	1.11			4.56	1.33			6.58	0.52			6.27	1.37		
3. Neatness of Employees	BO	6.16	0.63	0.98	11.48***	6.29	0.55	0.85	9.59***	5.87	1.35	0.89	5.45***	6.97	0.19	0.02	0.35	6.53	0.51	-0.13	-1.03
	BC	5.18	0.72			5.44	0.80			4.98	1.32			6.95	0.22			6.65	0.72		
4. Communication material	BO	5.99	0.08	-0.88	6.72 ***	5.97	0.71	0.77	7.20***	5.71	0.92	0.96	5.76***	6.31	0.54	-0.58	-7.25***	6.45	0.60	-0.30	2.58***
	BC	5.11	1.18			5.20	0.95			4.75	1.55			6.89	0.32			6.75	0.63		
Tangibility (01+02+03+04)	BO	23.13	2.21	5.28	18.46***	23.20	2.14	4.15	13.17***	23.30	2.60	4.25	9.07***	25.79	1.37	-1.14	-4.75***	25.07	1.57	-0.89	-1.44
	BC	17.84	2.37			19.04	2.78			19.05	4.33			26.93	1.06			25.97	3.79		

E&P denotes customer expectations and perceptions respectively. *P<0.01; ** P< 0.05; *** P<0.10

Bank:	SBI	PNB	JKB	CB	SCGB
Number: BC:	197	201	199	99	104
BO:	99	101	101	29	40
df:	294	300	298	126	142

TABLE 5.8

Customer Expectations and Perceptions about Reliability

Elements of Service Quality Dimension (Reliability)	Group	SBI Mean	SBI STD. Dev.	SBI M.D.	SBI T. Value	PNB Mean	PNB STD. Dev.	PNB M.D.	PNB T. Value	JKB Mean	JKB STD. Dev.	JKB M.D.	JKB T. Value	CB Mean	CB STD. Dev.	CB M.D.	CB T. Value	SCGB Mean	SCGB STD. Dev.	SCGB M.D.	SCGB T. Value
5. Promise to do something by a certain time, doing it	BO	6.06	0.71			6.19	0.64			6.27	0.63			6.14	0.35			6.45	0.60		
				0.46	3.92***			0.59	6.85***			1.28	8.51****			-0.29	-2.89***			-0.04	0.40
	BC	5.60	1.05			5.60	0.74			4.98	1.44			6.42	0.50			6.49	0.52		
6. Being sincere in solving the problem	BO	6.32	0.67			6.28	0.65			6.54	0.57			6.97	0.19			6.90	0.30		
				0.69	5.54***			0.63	6.28***			1.45	8.98***			0.50	5.06***			0.25	2.66***
	BC	5.63	1.15			5.65	0.89			5.09	1.57			6.46	0.52			6.65	0.55		
7. Performing the service right the first time	BO	6.13	0.74			6.16	0.50			6.24	0.85			6.21	0.41			6.50	0.60		
				0.58	4.66***			0.56	5.96***			1.20	8.06***			-0.36	-3.53***			-0.05	-0.55
	BC	5.55	1.13			5.60	0.87			5.04	1.36			6.57	0.50			6.56	0.54		
8. Providing the service at the promised time	BO	6.02	0.67			6.20	0.62			5.76	1.19			6.03	0.19			6.23	0.53		
				0.31	2.82***			0.49	5.40***			0.79	4.57***			-0.09	-1.47			-0.21	-2.14**
	BC	5.71	1.00			5.71	0.79			4.97	1.51			6.13	0.34			6.43	0.52		
9. Keeping records correctly	BO	6.85	0.36			6.87	0.34			6.53	0.76			6.97	0.19			6.78	0.53		
				0.39	4.09***			0.31	5.13***			0.81	4.88***			-0.02	-0.92			-0.21	-3.66***
	BC	6.46	0.92			6.56	0.56			5.72	1.58			6.99	0.10			6.98	0.14		
Reliability (05+06+07+08+09)	BO	31.37	2.16			33.69	1.72			31.34	2.77			32.31	0.76			32.85	1.90		
			2.43	4.88**			2.57	7.46***			5.53	8.48***			-0.26	-1.50			-0.26	-0.88	
	BC	28.94	4.69			29.11	3.23			25.81	6.24			32.57	0.85			33.11	1.48		

Note: Refer to Table 5.1 for details related to E & P, level of significance, N and df .

TABLE 5.9

Comparative Perceptions of Bank Officers and Customers about Responsiveness

Elements of Service Quality Dimension (Responsiveness	Group	SBI Mean	SBI STD. Dev.	SBI M.D.	SBI T. Value	PNB Mean	PNB STD. Dev.	PNB M.D.	PNB T. Value	JKB Mean	JKB STD. Dev.	JKB M.D.	JKB T. Value	CB Mean	CB STD. Dev.	CB M.D.	CB T. Value	SCGB Mean	SCGB STD. Dev.	SCGB M.D.	SCGB T. Value
10. Telling customers exactly when services will be performed	BO	6.11	0.62	0.73	6.53***	6.01	0.52	0.51	5.41***	6.13	0.65	1.15	7.76***	6.21	0.41	-0.13	-1.21	6.40	0.50	-0.06	-0.14
	BC	5.39	1.01			5.50	0.87			4.98	1.41			6.33	0.52			6.46	0.52		
11. Employees providing prompt service to customers	BO	5.86	0.88	1.20	7.72***	5.52	1.08	0.73	4.80***	6.26	0.76	1.52	8.44***	6.21	0.41	0.09	0.71	6.73	0.45	0.21	1.73*
	BC	4.65	1.42			4.79	1.33			4.74	1.72			6.11	0.68			6.52	0.70		
12. Employees who are always willing to help	BO	6.10	0.74	0.92	6.47***	5.89	0.92	0.67	5.14***	6.50	0.56	1.62	9.37***	6.79	0.41	0.46	3.43***	6.63	0.49	0.06	0.60
	BC	5.18	1.32			5.22	1.14			4.87	1.69			6.33	0.69			6.56	0.64		
13. Employees who are never too busy to respond to customers requests	BO	5.31	1.24	0.80	4.70***	5.40	1.11	0.86	5.31***	5.43	1.47	0.78	4.18***	6.28	0.45	0.24	1.59*	6.60	0.50	0.24	1.99**
	BC	4.52	1.43			4.54	1.42			4.65	1.55			6.04	0.75			6.36	0.71		
Responsiveness (10+11+12+13)	BO	23.38	2.66	3.64	7.21***	22.82	2.94	2.77	5.91***	24.31	2.59	5.06	8.41***	25.48	0.94	0.66	1.97**	26.35	1.18	0.45	1.32
	BC	19.73	4.65			20.04	4.22			19.24	5.73			24.81	1.73			25.89	2.03		

Note: Refer table 5.7 for details related to BO, CO, level of significance, N, and df .

TABLE 5.10

Comparative Perceptions of Bank Officers and Customers about Assurance

Elements of Service Quality Dimension (Assurance)	Group	SBI Mean	SBI STD. Dev.	SBI M.D.	SBI T. Value	PNB Mean	PNB STD. Dev.	PNB M.D.	PNB T. Value	JKB Mean	JKB STD. Dev.	JKB M.D.	JKB T. Value	CB Mean	CB STD. Dev.	CB M.D.	CB T. Value	SCGB Mean	SCGB STD. Dev.	SCGB M.D.	SCGB T. Value
14. Employees who are trustworthy	BO	6.04	0.53	0.73	5.89***	6.02	0.58	0.70	6.46***	6.24	0.59	1.17	7.16***	6.24	0.44	0.09	0.79	6.38	0.49	-0.21	-1.90**
	BC	5.31	1.17			5.32	1.01			5.07	1.59			6.15	0.56			6.59	0.63		
15. Feeling safe in transacting with the Banks	BO	6.88	0.33	0.26	3.70***	6.80	0.42	0.28	0.36***	6.72	0.51	0.63	4.49***	6.97	0.19	-2.02	-0.92	6.88	0.33	-0.09	-2.02**
	BC	6.62	0.66			6.52	0.70			6.09	1.36			6.99	0.10			6.97	0.22		
16. Employees who are consistently courteous	BO	6.12	0.69	1.09	8.22***	5.93	0.79	0.88	7.15***	6.26	0.576	1.14	7.66***	6.48	0.51	0.70	5.90***	6.63	0.49	0.14	1.37
	BC	5.03	1.22			5.05	1.10			5.12	1.44			5.78	0.58			6.48	0.59		
17. Employees who have the knowledge to answer the customers questions	BO	6.05	0.63	0.81	6.60***	6.01	1.03	0.81	6.59***	6.34	0.53	1.14	7.86***	6.24	0.44	0.75	4.32***	6.63	0.59	0.54	3.43***
	BC	5.24	1.14			5.20	0.99			5.20	1.40			549	0.90			6.09	0.93		
Assurance (14+15+16+17)	BO	25.09	1.64	2.89	7.58***	24.76	2.20	2.66	7.44***	25.55	1.52	4.08	8.29***	25.93	0.70	1.51	5.43***	26.50	1.37	0.37	1.17
	BC	22.19	3.60			22.09	3.24			21.47	4.82			24.41	1.44			26.12	1.83		

Note: Refer table 5.7 for details related to BO, CO, level of significance, N, and df.

TABLE 5.11

Comparative Perceptions of Bank Officers and Customers about Assurance

Elements of Service Quality Dimension (Assurance)	Group	SBI Mean	SBI STD. Dev.	SBI M.D.	SBI T. Value	PNB Mean	PNB STD. Dev.	PNB M.D.	PNB T. Value	JKB Mean	JKB STD. Dev.	JKB M.D.	JKB T. Value	CB Mean	CB STD. Dev.	CB M.D.	CB T. Value	SCGB Mean	SCGB STD. Dev.	SCGB M.D.	SCGB T. Value
18. Bank that give individual attention	BO	6.02	0.68	0.74	5.69***	6.06	0.72	0.74	6.34***	6.26	0.64	1.33	7.81***	6.28	0.45	-0.01	0.15	6.58	0.59	0.15	1.31
	BC	5.28	1.19			5.32	1.05			4.92	1.65			6.29	0.56			6.42	0.63		
19. Convenient operating hours	BO	6.23	0.88	1.38	8.12***	6.11	0.81	1.45	9.48***	6.18	0.89	1.63	9.12***	7.00	0.00	0.12	1.98**	6.70	0.46	-0.14	-1.20
	BC	4.85	1.57			4.66	1.43			4.55	1.67			6.88	0.33			6.84	0.66		
20. Employees who give personal attention	BO	6.16	0.60	0.99	7.51***	6.02	0.65	0.83	7.16***	6.27	0.65	1.40	8.22***	6.21	0.41	0.15	1.57*	6.65	0.48	0.25	1.96**
	BC	5.17	1.24			5.19	1.07			4.86	1.65			6.06	0.45			6.40	0.73		
21. Bank which has your best interests at least	BO	6.24	0.67	1.25	9.84***	6.17	0.66	1.28	10.54***	6.40	0.69	1.67	10.27***	7.00	.00	2.36	11.82***	6.78	0.42	1.04	5.70***
	BC	4.99	1.17			4.89	1.13			4.73	1.55			4.64	1.07			5.73	1.13		
22. Employees who under-stand specific needs of the customers	BO	5.98	0.68	1.14	8.32***	5.94	0.61	1.19	9.76***	6.22	0.61	1.41	8.95***	6.62	0.49	1.47	-9.64***	6.53	0.51	0.49	3.21***
	BC	4.84	1.28			4.75	1.14			4.81	1.52			5.15	0.77			6.04	0.90		
Empathy (18+19+20+21+22)	BO	30.63	2.37	5.49	9.59***	30.29	2.25	5.49	10.17***	31.31	2.34	7.43	10.49***	33.10	0.90	4.08	10.92***	33.22	1.73	1.7	3.24***
	BC	25.13	5.47			24.80	5.18			23.87	6.91			29.02	1.94			31.43	3.32		

Note: Refer table 5.7 for details related to BO, CO, level of significance, N, and df.

TABLE 5.12

Comparative Perceptions of Bank Officers and Customers about Overall Service Quality in Banks

Overall Service Quality	*Group*	*BANKS*																			
		SBI				*PNB*				*JKB*				*CB*				*SCGB*			
		Mean	*STD. Dev.*	*M.D.*	*T. Value*	*Mean*	*STD. Dev.*	*M.D.*	*T. Value*	*Mean*	*STD. Dev.*	*M.D.*	*T. Value*	*Mean*	*STD. Dev.*	*M.D.*	*T. Value*	*Mean*	*STD. Dev.*	*M.D.*	*T. Value*
Overall	BO	133.52	8.64			132.78	8.01			135.82	9.23			142.62	2.62			144.00	6.21		
Service				19.65	10.37***			17.66	10.43***			26.36	10.69***			4.85	5.84***			1.46	0.85
Quality	CO	113.86	17.72			115.11	16.01			109.45	23.73			137.76	4.23			142.53	10.10		

Note: Refer table 5.7 for details related to BO, CO, level of significance, N, and df.

6

Service Quality: Cross Banking Analysis

This chapter, besides discussing the empirical findings of the study regarding service quality variation among sample organizations, makes a comparative analysis of service quality between public sector and foreign banks, public sector and private sector banks, and private sector and foreign banks.

Service Quality Variation: A Comparative Analysis

The third objective of the study was to make a comparison across private and public sector banks as also national and foreign banks operating in India on critical service quality dimensions. To achieve this objective, mean values and standard deviation for each element of SERVQUAL and for each bank were computed separately to understand variation in service quality among sample organisation. One-way ANOVA was also performed for each elements of service quality to know exactly the extent of variation in service quality. The results obtained from this computation are presented in five tables (Table 6.1-6.5), each table showing results of related dimensions of service quality.

Tangibility

It is evident from table 6.1 that service quality of sample organisation varies considerably from each other on tangibility (50.84 per cent). The data clearly shows that foreign banks

TABLE 6.1

Service Quality Variation: Tangibility

Elements of Service Quality	*Banks*	*Mean values of service quality*	*Standard Deviation*	*Variation*			*F. Value*
				Between	*Total*	*Percent*	
	SBI	-2.64	1.02				
1. Up-to-date	PNB	-2.41	1.00				
Equipments	JKB	-1.75	1.61	617.187	1691.555	36.48	114.175*
	CB	-1.75	0.52				
	SCGB	-0.45	1.12				
	SBI	-3.31	1.08				
2. Physical	PNB	-2.38	1.19	985.068	2126.395	46.32	171.539*
Facilities	JKB	-1.86	1.48				
	CB	-0.31	0.75				
	SCGB	-0.52	1.26				
	SBI	-1.79	0.73				
3. Neatness of	PNB	-1.52	0.81	353.636	1027.920	34.40	104.237*
Employees	JKB	-1.61	0.41				
	CB	0.00	0.29				
	SCGB	-0.27	0.61				
	SBI	-1.84	1.16				
4. Communication	PNB	-1.74	0.99	428.304	1409.889	30.37	86.722*
Material	JKB	-1.70	1.54				
	CB	-0.01	0.44				
	SCGB	-0.15	0.59				
	SBI	-9.58	2.55				
Tangibility	PNB	-8.58	2.89	8815.852	17339.789	50.84	205.557*
	JKB	-6.93	4.69				
	CB	-0.66	1.16				
	SCGB	-1.39	3.25				

* $P < 0.001$

	Between Banks	Total
df	4	799
	N	800

(CB followed by SCGB) SERVQUAL score is high on tangibility while as Indian banks (SBI followed by PNB) SERVQUAL score is low on said dimension. However, JKB figures in between the two extremes. The element-wise analysis of tangibility shows that CB (-.33) figures highest on service quality while as SBI (-2.64) followed by PNB (-2.41) are lowest as far as up-to-date equipments in the bank are concerned. The position of JKB on this element is in between the two extremes.

The variation in service quality among the banks is 36.48 per cent, which is significant at .01 level of confidence. The data reveals that physical facilities available in a bank show very poor position of SBI followed by PNB whereas CB (-.31) emerged very high on this element. The variation on this element of service quality goes up to the level of 46.32 percent. CB continues to dominate its position as far as neatness of employees are concerned. Regarding communication material, the position of Indian banks shows minor variation. Foreign banks are meeting the expectations of their customers on this element as the negative variation is too low. Over all service quality on this element varies only 30.37 percent among the banks.

Reliability

Analysis of Table 6.2 reveals that variation on reliability among sample organisation is 18.27 per cent, which is relatively very low as compared to tangibility (50.84 percent, Table 6.1). The element-wise analysis of reliability brings to light that variation among the sample organisation is highest (16.12 per cent) as far as promise to do something by a certain time is concerned. However, the variation among the sample organisation is lowest on providing the service at promised time (9.34 per cent). The variation on the remaining elements of reliability varies from 11.13 per cent to 14.17 per cent among the sample organisations.

TABLE 6.2

Service Quality Variation: Reliability

Elements of Service Quality	*Banks*	*Mean values of service quality*	*Standard Deviation*	*Variation Between*	*Total*	*Percent*	*F. Value*
5. Promise to do something by a certain time, doing it	SBI	-1.22	1.05				
	PNB	-1.13	0.78				
	JKB	-1.51	1.54	172.221	1068.339	16.12	38.197*
	CB	-0.32	0.68				
	SCGB	-0.22	0.64				
6. Being sincere in solving the problem	SBI	-1.19	1.14				
	PNB	-1.10	1.93				
	JKB	-1.42	1.78	139.955	1256.969	11.13	24.902*
	CB	-0.44	0.59				
	SCGB	-0.21	0.53				
7. Performing the service right the first time	SBI	-1.19	1.13				
	PNB	-1.09	0.87				
	JKB	-1.36	1.69	171.900	1212.899	14.17	32.820*
	CB	0.23	0.65				
	SCGB	-0.12	0.56				
8. Providing the service at promised time	SBI	-1.14	0.98				
	PNB	-1.07	0.87				
	JKB	-1.48	1.72	102.002	1092.000	9.34	20.478*
	CB	-0.69	0.53				
	SCGB	-0.36	0.59				
9. Keeping records correctly	SBI	-0.48	0.82				
	PNB	-0.40	0.58				
	JKB	-0.94	1.54	91.585	710.195	12.89	29.425*
	CB	-0.03	0.22				
	SCGB	-0.22	0.14				
Reliability	SBI	-5.23	4.40				
	PNB	-4.79	3.21				
	JKB	-6.71	6.41	3227.523	17661.849	18.27	44.441*
	CB	-1.66	1.41				
	SCGB	-0.92	1.52				

Note: For details regarding level of significance, number and df refer table No.6.1

Responsiveness

It is evident from the data (Table 6.3) that variation in service quality on responsiveness among the sample organisations is 22.07 per cent. The element-wise analysis of responsiveness reveals highest variation (21.69 per cent) on employee providing prompt service to customers. Foreign banks, backed by banking technology, figure high on SERVQUAL score while as Indian banks figure too low on said element of service quality (responsiveness) as is evident from respective mean SERVQUAL scores. The variation among the sample organisations is low (14.90 per cent) on telling customers exactly when services will be performed. The SERVQUAL scores of Indian banks understudy is comparatively low against foreign banks on employee business to respond to customers request. The fact is that in the absence of relevant banking technology, front-line-staff will remain busy in processing volumes of financial transactions that take place everyday and it is hard to find time for them to attend customer requests. Foreign banks understudy on the other hand score high on the said element of responsiveness as they are backed by sophisticated banking technology. This is evident from respective mean SERVQUAL scores of sample organisation.

TABLE 6.3

Service Quality Variation: Responsiveness

Elements of Service Quality	*Banks*	*Mean values of service quality*	*Standard Deviation*	*Variation*			
				Between	*Total*	*Percent*	*F. Value*
10. Telling customers exactly when services will be performed	SBI	-1.47	1.03				
	PNB	-1.19	0.93				
	JKB	-1.43	1.55	161.652	1084.755	14.90	34.805*
	CB	-0.42	0.59				
	SCGB	-0.30	0.56				

11. Employees providing prompt service to customers	SBI	-2.23	1.45				
	PNB	-2.03	1.29				
	JKB	-1.95	1.75	402.675	1856.220	21.69	55.060*
	CB	-0.68	0.75				
	SCGB	-0.28	0.65				
12. Employees who are never too busy to respond to customers requests	SBI	-1.73	1.34				
	PNB	-1.60	1.16				
	JKB	-1.76	1.83	257.677	1655.689	15.56	36.633*
	CB	0.53	0.76				
	SCGB	-0.29	0.72				
13. Employees who are never too busy to respond to customers requests	SBI	-1.62	1.13				
	PNB	-1.59	1.02				
	JKB	-1.61	1.66	370.480	2039.189	18.16	44.126*
	CB	-0.74	0.65				
	SCGB	-0.32	0.69				
Responsiveness	SBI	-7.69	4.68				
	PNB	-7.08	4.09				
	JKB	-6.80	6.08	4455.531	20184.220	22.07	56.301*
	CB	-2.45	1.99				
	SCGB	-1.29	1.92				

Note: For details regarding level of significance, number and df refer table No.6.1

Assurance

The data in Table 6.4 provides information regarding variation in service quality on assurance among the sample organisation and brings to light that variation on assurance is 13.93 per cent only. Element-wise analysis on assurance brings to light highest variation (14.67 per cent) on employees trustworthiness while as variation is lowest (5.08 per cent) on employees knowledge to answer customer questions. The SERVQUAL scores of sample organisations also do not exhibit much variation on employees' knowledge to answer customer questions. All banks, however, emerged strong comparatively on feeling safe in transacting with the bank, though JKB scored relatively low on this element of assurance.

TABLE 6.4

Service Quality Variation: Assurance

Elements of Service Quality	*Banks*	*Mean values of service quality*	*Standard Deviation*	*Variation*			
				Between	*Total*	*Percent*	*F. Value*
14. Employees who are trustworthy	SBI	-1.62	1.13				
	PNB	-1.59	1.02				
	JKB	-1.61	1.66	187.719	1279.555	14.67	34.171*
	CB	-0.74	0.65				
	SCGB	-0.32	0.69				
15. Feeling safe in transacting with the bank	SBI	-0.31	0.64				
	PNB	-0.39	0.71				
	JKB	-0.50	1.12	31.939	477.555	6.68	14.245*
	CB	-0.02	0.20				
	SCGB	-0.04	0.37				
16. Employees Who are consistently courteous	SBI	-1.83	1.27				
	PNB	-1.79	1.12				
	JKB	-1.39	1.55	191.952	1319.795	14.54	33.826*
	CB	-1.09	0.67				
	SCGB	-0.35	0.65				
17. Employees who have the knowledge to answer cust-omers question	SBI	-1.55	1.21				
	PNB	-1.60	0.99				
	JKB	-1.28	1.36	64.723	1115.755	5.80	12.239*
	CB	-1.34	1.01				
	SCGB	-0.70	1.00				
Assurance	SBI	-5.31	3.55				
	PNB	-5.37	3.16				
	JKB	-4.78	4.64	1518.956	10899.520	13.93	32.183*
	CB	-3.15	1.72				
	SCGB	-1.33	1.88				

Note: For details regarding level of significance, number and df refer table No.6.1

Empathy

The analysis of table 6.5 reveals that variation in service quality, among sample organisation, on empathy is 14.25 per cent. Mean SERVQUAL scores of foreign banks (SCGB followed by CB) are comparatively hig against Indian banks.

The element-wise analysis of empathy brings to light highest variation (27.58 per cent) on convenient operating hours while as the variation is lowest (4.89 per cent) in respect of banks which have your best interests at heart. Foreign banks backed by banking technology expectedly score high on convenient operating hours as against Indian banks. Banking technology is one of the important strategic mean which helps foreign bankers to score high on banks that gives individual attention to customers, convenient operating hours and employees who give personal attention to their customers. The variations on these elements of empathy are 12.56, 27.58 and 11.34 per cent respectively.

TABLE 6.5

Service Quality Variation: Empathy

Elements of Service Quality	*Banks*	*Mean values of service quality*	*Standard Deviation*	*Variation*			
				Between	*Total*	*Percent*	*F. Value*
18. Bank that gives individual attention to customers	SBI	-1.55	1.55				
	PNB	-1.51	1.09				
	JKB	-1.48	1.70	166.962	1328.499	12.56	*28.569
	CB	-0.57	0.67				
	SCGB	-0.38	0.69				
19. Convenient operating hours	SBI	-2.09	1.53				
	PNB	-2.27	1.47				
	JKB	-1.93	1.85	615.689	2231.699	27.58	*75.722
	CB	-0.08	0.40				
	SCGB	-0.12	0.58				
20. Employees who gives personal attent-ion their customers	SBI	-1.68	1.26				
	PNB	-1.58	1.11				
	JKB	-1.45	1.82	167.273	1474.249	11.34	*25.437
	CB	-0.77	0.60				
	SCGB	-0.37	0.72				
21. Bank which has your best interest at	SBI	-1.80	1.25				
	PNB	-1.88	1.19				
	JKB	-1.56	1.63	69.430	1418.955	4.89	*10.225

heart	CB	-2.28	1.10				
	SCGB	-1.21	1.07				
22. Employees who understand specific needs of the customer	SBI	-1.94	1.33				
	PNB	-1.98	1.14				
	JKB	-1.58	1.48	101.573	1295.555	7.84	*16.908
	CB	-1.83	0.81				
	SCGB	-0.88	0.93				
Empathy	SBI	-9.06	5.41				
	PNB	-9.21	5.27				
	JKB	-8.01	6.82	3646.761	25589.389	14.25	33.031*
	CB	-5.53	2.23				
	SCGB	-2.95	3.03				

Note: For details regarding level of significance, number and df refer table No.6.1

Table 6.6 presents data regarding dimension-wise variation in service quality among the banks and highlights that variation among the banks on tangibility dimension is highest i.e., (50.84) per cent followed by responsiveness (22.07 percent). The variation on service quality dimensions except tangibility varies from 13.93 to 22.07 percent among the sample organisation. This is an important finding for Indian banks, which suggests substantial investment on tangibility to improve service quality. All Indian banks particularly SBI followed by PNB and JKB, with high negative mean scores, highlight their poor position on tangibility. The total variation among banks on this dimension is 50.84 per cent, which is significant at .001 level of confidence. The Table 16.6 reveals that the banks do not show much variation on assurance. The low variation in mean scores among Indian banks shows greater homogeneity on assurance dimension. SCGB's low negative mean score (–1.33) reveals that the bank scores high on this dimension in comparison to other banks. The data on remaining dimensions of service quality (reliability, responsiveness and empathy) reveals low variations (18.27, 22.07 and 14.25 percent respectively) among the banks.

TABLE 6.6

Service Quality Variation: Dimension-Wise

Element of Service Quality	*Banks*	*Mean values of service quality*	*Standard Devi-ation*	*VARIATION Between banks*	*Total*	*Percent Explained*	*F. Value*
	SBI	-9.58	2.55				
	PNB	-8.50	2.89				
Tangibility	JKB	-6.93	4.69	8815.852	17339.789	50.84	205.557*
	CB	-0.66	1.16				
	SCGB	-1.39	3.25				
	SBI	-5.23	4.40				
	PNB	-4.79	3.21				
Reliability	JKB	-6.71	6.41	3227.523	17661.849	18.27	44.441*
	CB	-1.66	1.41				
	SCGB	-0.92	1.52				
	SBI	-7.69	4.68				
	PNB	-7.08	4.09				
Responsiveness	JKB	-6.80	6.08	4455.531	20184.220	22.07	56.301*
	CB	-2.45	1.99				
	SCGB	-1.29	1.92				
	SBI	-5.31	3.55				
	PNB	-5.37	3.16				
Assurance	JKB	-4.78	4.64	1518.956	10899.520	13.93	32.183*
	CB	-3.15	1.72				
	SCGB	-1.33	1.88				
	SBI	-9.06	5.41				
	PNB	-9.21	5.27				
Empathy	JKB	-8.01	6.82	3646.761	25589.389	14.25	33.031*
	CB	-5.53	2.23				
	SCGB	-2.95	3.03				

Note: For details regarding level of significance, number and df refer table No.6.1

Table 6.7 summarizes data regarding overall variation in service quality among the sample organization and brings to light that overall variation among the banks varies to the extent of 29.62 per cent. The highest negative mean scores of SBI (-36.88) followed by PNB (-34.95) reveals that these two banks are poor in service quality in comparison to other banks understudy. In the same way the data on table 6.6 reveals that SCGB followed by CB with relatively low mean scores (-7.08 and –13.44) show that these two banks are high in service quality in comparison to other banks under study. The JKBs' mean score (-33.23) reveals that the bank is positioned in between the two extremes.

TABLE 6.7

Service Quality Variation: Overall

Service Quality	*Banks*	*Mean values of service quality*	*Standard Deviation*	*VARIATION*			*F. Value*
				Between banks	*Total*	*Percent Explained*	
	SBI	-36.88	17.05				
	PNB	-34.95	15.59				
Service Quality	JKB	-33.23	23.02	93220.475	314724.7	29.62	*83.644
	CB	-13.44	6.05				
	SCGB	-7.88	8.48				

Note: For details regarding level of significance, number and df refer table No.6.1

It is disheartening to note that there is no research evidence available in India on service quality variation in banks. Present study will certainly fill up the gap. Table 6.6 highlights dimension-wise service quality variation in the sample organisation and brings to light that service quality variation among the banks is high on tangibility followed by responsiveness while as variation is low on assurance followed by empathy. These findings make it clear that those foreign banks under study which are backed by sophisticated technology score high on tangibility and responsiveness, because tangibility has a direct bearing on responsiveness. In other words these findings suggest heavy investment in technology for Indian banks. The future of banks lies in technology, which will obviously lead to faster and better customer service.

Service Quality in Public Sector and Foreign Banks

To measure service quality between public sector and foreign banks, mean values of service quality and standard deviation were computed separately for two public sector and two foreign banks. This followed T. test to determine level of difference in service quality between two sectors. The results obtained from this analysis are presented in Table 6.8. The data highlights a visible difference in service quality between public sector and foreign banks in all elements of service quality except for one element (i.e., banks which has your best interests at heart) in which difference is almost negligible. This difference between public sector and foreign banks is significant at .01 level of confidence.

Table 6.8

Element-wise Service Quality In Public Sector and Foreign Banks

Elements of Service Quality		*Group*	*Mean SURVQ-UAL Score*	*Standard Deviation*	*Mean Difference*	*T. Values*
01	Up-to-date Equipments	PB	-2.53	1.02	-2.14	-25.38*
		FB	-0.39	0.88		
02	Physical Facilities	PB	-3.07	1.16	-2.65	-27.78*
		FB	-0.42	0.99		
03	Employees are well dressed and neat appearing	PB	-1.66	0.78	-1.52	-25.20*
		FB	-0.14	0.50		
04	Communication Material	PB	-1.79	1.08	-1.71	-21.30*
		FB	-0.08	0.52		
05	Promise to do something by a certain time, doing it	PB	-1.18	0.93	-0.91	-12.41*
		FB	-0.27	0.66		
06	Being sincere in solving the problem	PB	-1.15	1.04	-0.82	10.49*
		FB	-0.33	0.57		

07.	Performing the service right the first time	PB	-1.14	1.01	-0.97	-12.55*
		FB	-0.17	0.61		
08	Providing the service at the promised time	PB	-1.11	0.92	-0.59	-8.26*
		FB	-0.52	0.58		
09	Keeping records correctly	PB	-0.44	0.71	-0.40	-8.81*
		FB	-0.04	0.19		
10	Telling customers exactly when services will be performed	PB	-1.33	0.99	-0.97	-12.90*
		FB	-0.36	0.57		
11	Employees providing prompt service to customers	PB	-2.13	1.38	-1.66	-16.06*
		FB	-0.47	0.73		
12	Employees who are always willing to help	PB	1.66	1.66	-1.26	-13.14*
		FB	0.40	0.75		
13	Employees who are never too busy to respond to customers requests	PB	-2.26	1.45	-1.64	-15.03*
		FB	-0.62	0.79		
14	Employees who are trustworthy	PB	-1.61	1.07	-1.09	-13.04*
		FB	-0.52	0.70		
15	Feeling safe in transacting with the bank	PB	-0.35	0.67	-1.26	-13.14*
		FB	-0.02	0.30		
16	Employees who are consistently courteous	PB	1.81	1.19	-1.10	-11.97*
		FB	-0.71	0.76		
17	Employees who have the knowledge to answer customers questions	PB	-1.57	1.10	-0.47	-5.95*
		FB	-1.10	1.06		
18	Bank that gives individual attention	PB	-1.53	-1.53	-1.06	-12.38*
		FB	-0.47	0.68		
19	Convenient operating hours	PB	-2.18	1.50	-2.09	-19.20*
		FB	-0.09	0.50		

20	Employees who give personal attention	PB	-1.63	1.19	-1.07	-11.80*
		FB	-0.56	0.70		
21	Bank which has your best interests at heart	PB	-1.84	1.22	-0.11	-1.00
		FB	-1.73	1.21		
22	Employees who understand specific needs of the customer	PB	-1.96	1.24	-0.62	-6.16*
		FB	-1.34	0.99		

Note: Banking Sector (PB) Number df. * P< 0.01, ** P < 0.05, *** P < 0.10.

Banking Sector (PB)	Number	df.
Foreign Banks (FB)	398	599
Private Banks (PB)	203	

TABLE 6.9

Dimension-wise Service Quality in Public Sector and Foreign Banks

Dimensions of Service Quality	*Group*	*Mean SURVQUAL Score*	*Standard Deviation*	*Mean Difference*	*T. Values*
Tangibility	PB	-9.04	2.78	-8.01	-34.59*
	FB	-1.03	2.48		
Reliability	PB	-5.01	3.85	-3.73	-13.26*
	FB	-1.28	1.52		
Responsiveness	PB	-7.38	4.40	-5.52	-16.99*
	FB	-1.86	2.04		
Assurance	PB	-5.34	3.36	-3.12	-12.18*
	FB	-2.22	2.02		
Empathy	PB	-9.14	5.33	-4.93	-12.23*
	FB	-4.21	2.96		

Note: For details regarding Banking Sector, Banks, Number, df and Level of Significance refer Table No.6.8.

Table 6.9 presents data on dimensions of service quality between public sector and foreign banks. The data revels high negative mean values in tangibility followed by responsiveness of public sector banks which reflects a wide gap in said dimensions of service quality in comparison to foreign banks.

Table 6.10 summarizes data regarding overall quality of service in public sector and foreign banks. The data brings to light a significant gap between two sectors. The mean difference (– 25.31) in service quality between public sector and foreign banks shows a significant (P<0.01) degree of variation in quality of service offered by two sectors.

TABLE 6.10

Overall Service Quality in Public Sector and Foreign Banks

Overall Service Quality	*Group*	*Mean SERVQUAL Scores*	*Standard Deviation*	*Mean Difference*	*T. Values*
Overall Service Quality	FB	-35.91	16.34	-25.31	-20.86*
	PB	-10.60	7.89		

Note: For details regarding Banking Sector, Banks, Number, df., and Level of Significance refer Table No. 6.8.

Two major reasons can be identified for such high service quality variation: first, foreign banks are backed by state of art banking technology; second, foreign banks are operating in selected segments and offer selected services also. Banking technology helps in the delivery of quality service which covers features such as, speed, accuracy, promptness etc. In other words banking technology gives them a differential/ competitive edge in financial services. Secondly, the market share of public sector banks is 81.43% in deposits, 64.50% in advances; 90.50% in staff and 89.51% in branches (IBA Bulletin, 2002) which is indicative of widespread market operations and diversified services of public sector banks. This definitely tells upon the quality of service, as they are not able to handle large volumes of financial services, which take place every day in absence of banking technology. This fact is evident from high mean differences between two sectors on tangibles and responsiveness. Mean difference, between the two sectors, is high on empathy also. This is because foreign banks score high on certain elements of empathy, which are directly or indirectly connected with technology.

Service Quality in Public Sector and Private Sector Banks

To measure service quality between public sector and private sector banks, mean values of service quality and standard deviation were computed separately for two public sector banks and one private bank. Average mean values were calculated for public sector banks and compared with private bank. This process followed a T.Test to determine degree of difference in service quality between two different sectors. The results obtained from this analysis are presented in table 6.11. The elements wise analysis of service quality between public sector and private sector banks reveals that there are significant differences in fourteen elements of service quality, between the two sectors, which account for 63.63 per cent. The data highlights a wide gap in service quality between the two sectors as for as up-to-date equipment, physical facilities, correct record keeping and busied employees to respond to customers requests are concerned. Regarding other elements where difference in service quality exists between the two sectors, the difference gap in less them 50 percent. This follows that there is minor variation in service quality between public sector and private sector banks.

Table 6.11 presents information regarding dimension of service quality in public sector and private sector banks. The data clearly reveals that service quality across all dimensions except responsiveness varies significantly between the two sectors. The position of private sector banks is much better as far as tangibility and reliability is concerned as in evident frcm respective mean scores. However, the two sectors are at par as for as responsiveness is concerned.

TABLE 6.11

Element-wise Service Quality In Public Sector and Private Sector Banks

Elements of Service Quality	*Group*	*Mean SURVQ-UAL Score*	*Standard Deviation*	*Mean Difference*	*T. Values*
01 Up-to-date Equipments	PB	-2.53	1.02	-0.78	-7.12*
	PR	-1.75	1.61		
02 Physical Facilities	PB	-3.07	1.16	-1.21	-10.88*
	PR	-1.86	1.48		
03 Employees are well dressed and neat appearing	PB	-1.66	0.78	-0.05	-0.47
	PB	-1.61	1.41		
04 Communication Material	PB	-1.79	1.08	-0.09	-0.83
	PR	-1.70	1.54		
05 Promise to do something by a certain time, doing it	PB	-1.18	0.93	0.33	3.27*
	PR	-1.51	1.54		
06 Being sincere in solving the problem	PB	-1.15	1.04	0.27	2.39*
	PR	-1.42	1.78		
07 Performing the service right the first time	PB	-1.14	1.01	0.22	1.95**
	PR	-1.36	1.69		
08 Providing the service at the promised time	PB	-1.11	0.92	0.37	3.47*
	PR	-1.48	1.72		
09 Keeping records correctly	PB	-0.44	0.71	0.50	5.73*
	PR	-0.94	1.45		
10 Telling customers exactly when services will be performed	PB	-1.33	0.99	0.10	0.93
	PR	-1.43	1.55		

11	Employees providing prompt service to customers	PB	-2.13	1.38	-0.18	-1.37
		PR	-1.95	1.75		
12	Employees who are always willing to help	PB	-1.66	1.25	0.10	0.76
		PR	-1.76	1.83		
13	Employees who are never too busy to respond to customers requests	PB	-2.26	1.45	-0.60	-4.26*
		PB	-1.66	1.90		
14	Employees who are trustworthy	PB	-1.61	1.07	0.00	0.06
		PR	-1.61	1.66		
15	Feeling safe in transacting with the bank	PB	-0.35	0.67	0.15	2.04**
		PR	-0.50	1.12		
16	Employees who are consistently courteous	PB	-1.81	1.19	-0.42	-3.65*
		PR	-1.39	1.55		
17	Employees who have the knowledge to answer customers questions	PB	-1.57	1.10	-0.29	-2.86*
		PR	-1.28	1.36		
18	Bank that gives individual attention	PB	-1.53	1.12	-0.05	-0.43
		PR	-1.48	1.70		
19	Convenient operating hours	PB	-2.18	1.50	-0.25	-1.76***
		PR	-1.93	1.85		
20	Employees who give personal attention	PB	-1.63	1.19	-0.18	-1.46
		PR	-1.45	1.82		
21	Bank which has your best interests at heart	PB	-1.84	1.22	0.28	-2.36*
		PR	-1.56	1.63		
22	Employees who under-understand specific needs of the customer	PB	-1.96	1.24	-0.38	-3.26*
		PR	-1.58	1.48		

Note: Banking Sector (PB) Number df. * P< 0.01, ** P < 0.05, *** P < 0.10.

Banking Sector (PB)	Number	df.
Foreign Banks (FB)	203	400
Private Banks (PB)	199	

Table 6.11 presents information regarding dimension of service quality in public sector and private sector banks. The data clearly reveals that service quality across all dimensions except responsiveness varies significantly between the two sectors. The position of private sector banks is much better as far as tangibility and reliability is concerned as in evident from respective mean scores. However, the two sectors are at par as for as responsiveness is concerned.

TABLE 6.12

Dimension-wise Service Quality In Public Sector and Private Sector Banks

Dimensions of Service Quality	*Group*	*Mean SURVQUAL Score*	*Standard Deviation*	*Mean Difference*	*T. Values*
Tangibility	PB	-9.04	2.78	-2.11	-6.88*
	PR	-6.93	4.69		
Reliability	PB	-5.01	3.85	1.70	4.04*
	PR	-6.71	6.41		
Responsiveness	PB	-7.38	4.40	-0.58	-1.33
	PR	-6.80	6.08		
Assurance	PB	-5.34	3.36	-0.56	-1.67****
	PR	-4.78	4.64		
Empathy	PB	-9.14	5.33	-1.13	-2.21**
	PR	-8.01	6.82		

Note: For details regarding Banking Sector, Banks, Number, df., and Level of Significance refer Table No.6.11.

All respective service quality elements/dimensions of public sector and private sector banks were summed up (Table 6.13) with a view to examine over all variation in service quality, if any, between the two sectors. The table clearly reveals that over-all service quality varies significantly ($P < 0.10$) as is evident from mean difference -2.68, between the two sectors.

TABLE 6.13

Overall Service Quality in Public Sector and Private Sector Banks

Overall Service Quality	*Group Scores*	*Mean SERVQUAL*	*Standard Deviation*	*Mean Difference*	*T. Values*
Overall Service Quality	FB	-35.91	16.34	-2.68	-1.63***
	PB	-33.23	23.02		

***Note*:** For details regarding Banking Sector, Banks, Number, df., and Level of Significance refer Table No. 6.11.

Service Quality in Foreign and Private Sector Banks

Service quality mean scores and standard deviation were computed for two foreign banks and one private sector bank followed by a T. test with a view to study service quality variations, if any, between foreign and private banks. The results obtained from this computation are presented in Table 6.14. The table clearly reveals that there are significant

TABLE 6.14

Element-wise Service Quality in Foreign and Private Sector Banks

Elements of Service Quality	*Group*	*Mean SURVQ-UAL Score*	*Standard Deviation*	*Mean Difference*	*T. Values*
01 Up-to-date Equipments	FB	-0.39	0.88	1.36	10.53*
	PB	-1.75	1.61		
02 Physical Facilities	FB	-0.42	0.99	1.44	11.54*
	PB	-1.86	1.48		
03 Employees are well dressed and neat appearing	FB	-0.14	0.50	1.47	14.04*
	PB	-1.61	1.41		

04	Communication Material	FB	-0.08	0.52	1.62	14.15*
		PB	-1.70	1.54		
05	Promise to do something by a certain time, doing it	FB	-0.27	0.66	1.24	10.49*
		PB	-1.51	1.54		
06	Being sincere in solving the problem	FB	-0.33	0.57	1.09	8.34*
		PB	-1.42	1.78		
07	Performing the service right the first time	FB	-0.17	0.61	1.19	9.39*
		PB	-1.36	1.69		
08	Providing the service at the promised time	FB	-0.52	0.58	0.96	7.55*
		PB	-1.48	1.72		
09	Keeping records correctly	FB	-0.04	0.19	0.96	9.27*
		PB	-0.94	1.45		
10	Telling customers exactly when services will be performed	FB	-0.36	0.57	1.07	9.18*
		PB	-1.43	1.55		
11	Employees providing prompt service to customers	FB	0.47	0.73	1.48	11.08*
		PB	-1.95	1.75		
12	Employees who are always willing to help	FB	-0.40	0.75	1.36	9.73*
		PB	-1.76	1.83		
13	Employees who are never too busy to respond to customers requests	FB	-0.62	0.79	1.09	8.61*
		PB	-1.66	1.90		
14	Employees who are trustworthy	FB	-0.52	0.70	1.09	8.61*
		PB	-1.61	1.66		
15	Feeling safe in transacting with the bank	FB	-0.02	0.30	0.48	6.54*
		PB	-0.50	1.12		

16	Employees who are consistently courteous	FB	-0.71	0.76	0.68	5.63*
		PB	-1.39	1.55		
17	Employees who have the knowledge to answer customers questions	FB	-1.01	1.06	0.27	2.15**
		PB	-1.28	1.36		
18	Bank that gives individual attention	FB	-0.47	0.68	1.01	7.82*
		PB	-1.48	1.70		
19	Convenient operating hours	FB	-0.09	0.50	1.84	13.63*
		PB	-1.93	1.85		
20	Employees who give personal attention	FB	-0.56	0.70	0.89	6.48*
		PB	-1.45	1.82		
21	Bank which has your best interestsat heart	FB	-1.73	1.21	-0.17	-1.23
		PB	-1.56	1.63		
22	Employees who under-stand specific needs of the customer	FB	-1.34	0.99	0.24	1.93**
			-1.58	1.48		

Note:

Banking Sector (PB)	Number	df.	* P< 0.01, ** P < 0.05, *** P < 0.10.
Foreign Banks (FB)	203	400	
Private Banks (PB)	199		

differences (P < 0.01 and < 0.05) in all elements of service quality between foreign and private sector banks except element number twenty one (i.e., bank which has your best interests at heart) which shows negligible differences. The mean difference on all elements of SQ between two sectors highlights that difference of more than one and more than half accounts for 63.64 and 18 percent respectively.

Table 6.15 presents data regarding dimensions of service quality between foreign and private sector banks. As is evident from the data there exist significant differences (P < 0.01) in service quality between foreign and private sector banks, across all dimensions. The data clearly reveals a wide gap as far as tangibility followed by reliability and responsiveness are concerned as is evident from respective mean differences. However, the service quality gap is narrow as far as assurances followed by empathy are concerned.

TABLE 6.15

Dimension-wise Service Quality in Foreign and Private Sector Banks

Dimensions of Service Quality	*Group*	*Mean SURVQUAL Score*	*Standard Deviation*	*Mean Difference*	*T. Values*
Tangibility	FB	-1.03	2.48	5.90	15.78*
	PB	-6.93	4.69		
Reliability	FB	-1.28	1.52	5.43	11.74*
	PB	-6.71	6.41		
Responsiveness	FB	-1.86	2.04	4.94	10.96*
	PB	-6.80	6.08		
Assurance	FB	-2.22	2.02	2.56	7.22*
	PB	-4.78	4.64		
Empathy	FB	-4.21	2.96	3.80	7.26*
	PB	-8.01	6.82		

Note: For details regarding Banking Sector, Banks, Number, df., and Level of Significance refer Table No.6.14.

The data contained in Table 6.16 clearly reveals that there is a wide gap in the overall quality of services offered by foreign banks compared to private banks as is evident from mean difference (22.63). The T. value shows that the level of significant difference is 0.01.

TABLE 6.16

Overall Service Quality in Foreign and Private Banks

Overall Service Quality	*Group*	*Mean SERVQUAL Scores*	*Standard Deviation*	*Mean Difference*	*T. Values*
Overall Service Quality	FB	-10.60	7.89	22.63	13.23*
	PB	-33.23	23.02		

***Note*:** For details regarding Banking Sector, Banks, Number, df., and Level of Significance refer Table No.6.14.

7

Conclusions, Suggestions and Policy Implications

The tremendous growth of services sector has resulted in its increased importance to the world economies. In 1948, 54% of the GDP of United States was generated by services and at present 73% of the U.S. GDP(2001-02) comes from the services sector. In the Indian economy the services sector accounted for 28 percent of the GDP at constant prices in 1960-61 which increased to 31 per cent in 1970-71, 37 per cent in 1980-81 and 52 percent in 2000-01. The weight-age of services sector has been increasing in the overall GDP. Banking, insurance and transport are important service sectors, which have recorded very rapid growth, specifically in 1970s and 1980s. This growing share of services sector is an indication that in future, India's GDP growth will be influenced considerably by the services sector. The services sector in India has consistently out performed the rest of the economy in recent years, in response to the reform programmes undertaken since 1991. In fact, the response to liberalization has probably been more in service sector, partly because of lower fixed investment requirements. Moreover technological advances have made it possible for India to compete on a global basis in the areas such as software development and information services. Some of other potential areas for India include accountancy, health, education and banking services.

As the race to compete and survive intensifies, business firms discover their service offerings becoming dangerously similar to one another. The service products of airlines, banks, fast foods, and the like equally measure up to one another's specifications. Airlines offer identical flights with the same fare structure, banks offer virtually the same schemes on the same terms and conditions, and fast foodstuffs offer identical menus. How does, then, the customer patronize one and not the other? Of course his decisions are based on quality. Customers take into account the relative efficiency while choosing a particular service firm.

Customers are increasingly aware of alternatives on offer in relation to services and provider organisations and also of rising standards of service. Consequently expectations rise and consumers become more critical of the quality of service received, and so companies can never be complacent. In addition, knowledge of the costs and benefits of keeping customers relative to attracting new ones draws companies attention to looking after present customers, responding to their needs and problems, and developing long term relationships (Berry and Parasuraman, 1991; Gilmore and Carson, 1993; Gronroos, 1984, 1988; Parasuraman, et. al., 1985, 1992 and Susan and Dong, 1994). In today's increasingly competitive environment, quality service is critical to banks success.

With the above backdrop in view the present investigation, into a largely unexplored area, was undertaken to examine service quality in banks in Northern India and probe objectively into the factors that help or obstruct in achieving quality service and on the basis of the findings of the study offer policy recommendations for achieving much needed quality service in banks. The major focus of the study was to make a comparison among banks on service quality and identify factors for customer satisfaction/dissatisfaction.

Two public sector banks, two foreign banks and one private bank were selected for the present study keeping in view their role in shaping the economic destiny and in instrumentalising the process of social and economic transformation in Northern India. In terms of advances and deposits, employee strength and branch network, these banks stand at the top. The research approach employed consisted of literature survey and field study. The study relied much on primary data. For that purpose SERVQUAL Model (A Multiple – Item Scale for Measuring Consumer Perceptions of Service Quality) propounded by Parasuraman, et.al. (1988) was used. Through the SERVQUAL Model information on service quality was obtained both from bank customers and bank officials. For this purpose eight hundred bank customers, representing cross section of people and spread over Northern India were randomly selected. In the same way three hundred seventy bank officials in varied pay scales were selected. While choosing bank officials, the method of convenience sampling was used. Bank officials in varied pay scales were purposely selected as they have more influence, in their respective branch offices, in administering banking policies and procedures besides marketing of their services. The data thus collected was analysed and processed with the help of various statistical tools.

Based on the objectives of the study, the entire subject matter has been divided into seven broad chapters. An attempt has been made in the present chapter to recapitulate the major findings of the study with a view to draw conclusions and analyse critically the implications of these findings. Suggestions for better service quality in banks also feature in this chapter.

Conclusions

The analysis of service quality in banks clearly reveals that service quality of foreign banks is comparatively much better than Indian banks. The comparative SERVQUAL scores of banks reveals that SCGB followed by CB figure high on service quality while as SBI followed by PNB figure low on service quality. The JKB figures in between the two extremes (ranked 3rd).

Indian banks, particularly public sector banks are very poor on tangibles and responsiveness. Foreign banks especially CB having technological edge expectedly score high on tangibles and any further investment on said dimension, for the time being, will be waste of resources. Contrary to foreign banks, Indian banks, particularly public sector banks, are operating in all segments. Retail banking constitutes nearly eighty per cent of their total banking business. The absence of relevant banking technology, particularly inter-net and ATM's, which can take care of most of retail banking, is the main source of consumer dissatisfaction as far as tangibility and responsiveness dimensions of service quality are concerned.

The findings of the study lead us to the conclusion that there are severe deficiencies in tangibility particularly in physical facilities and up-to-date equipments among Indian banks. This research finding suggests substantial investment on tangibles, which will improve service quality to a great extent. The investment on tangibles particularly ATMs will reduce work load of front-line staff and will provide way to quick response.

Reliability emerged the most important service quality dimension for both banks as well as for bank customers. This research finding is in line with the research findings of Lewis, (1991) and Parasuraman (1985). Responsiveness, Tangibility, empathy and assurance emerged 2nd, 3rd, 4th and least important dimension respectively. It is also clear that customers of all the banks, under study, do not exhibit greater variation as far as importance to service quality dimensions are concerned. These research findings lead us to conclusion that banks have correct assessment, about their customers, on importance to service quality dimensions.

The analysis of service quality in banks across income demographic variable shows that service quality of Indian banks as perceived by their respective customers varies (high/low) as their level of income varies (high/low). However, it is not necessary that service quality will be proportionately high/low to the level of income. Contrary to Indian banks, there is minor variation in service quality across different income groups among foreign banks for one simple reason – i.e., they operate mostly through ATM's, which cannot recognize any difference in levels of income.The analysis of service quality in banks as perceived by different age groups reveals that service quality in all banks is comparatively better among higher age groups where as reverse is the case among lower age groups. The SERVQUAL score of banks, under study, shows relatively better service quality in banks as perceived by respective bank customers in region 3rd (Delhi) where as quite reverse is the case in region Ist (J&K State). The obvious reason for such a variation in service quality in different regions is the level of banking competition. As the level of competition intensifies, service quality also goes up. It is tough competition in which consumers generally get a fair deal. But unfortunately, no research evidence is available on service quality in different competitive regions to corroborate present research findings.

The SERVQUAL scores of banks, under study, as reported by business and service group customers reveal that banks provide comparatively better service quality to business group customers in comparison to service group customers. The obvious reason for this phenomenon is that they are comparatively small in number with comparatively high level of income as against to service group customers. This research finding supports one of the earlier research finding of the study. The SERVQUAL scores of banks as reported by respective respondents belonging to different education levels, do not exhibit greater variation in service quality. This finding leads us to the conclusion that banks do not recognize education as a factor to differentiate customers/markets like level of income or profession is used. But unfortunately, this research finding does not find any research support.

The analysis of importance to service quality dimensions as reported by all respective respondents, varying on demographic variables of sample organization, leads us to the conclusion that reliability is the most important service quality dimension followed by responsiveness. This research finding is in line with those of Hart (1988), Lewis (1991), Parasuraman, et.al. (1985, 1988, 1991). Berry, et.al. (1994) along with Zeithaml, et.al..(1990), while supporting the findings of above mentioned researchers about the most important service quality dimension, found tangibility followed by empathy as the least important service quality dimension. The finding of the present study reveals assurance as the least important dimension followed by empathy. Tangibility however, emerged third important service quality dimension.

Service quality is a measure of how well the service level delivered matches customer expectations. Delivering quality service means conforming to customer expectations on a consistent basis (Lewis and Booms, 1983). The findings of the study regarding customer expectations and perceptions reveal that Indian banks fall much below the expectations of their customers on all dimensions of service quality in comparison to foreign banks. This research finding is in line with the research findings of many scholars in India (Mankidy, 2000; Muniraj 1994; Nageswar and Pramod, 1990; Ramachandra, 1992 and Sundaram, 1982) and Practioners

(Middleton, 1994; Saraf, 1997; and Srinivas, 1996).Although little empirical evidence is available to support the findings of above mentioned scholars and practitioners. Foreign banks, including private banks and non-banking institutions, backed by banking technology have raised the aspirations of customers of other banks. In delivery of quality service, particularly in banks, it is speed, accuracy, promptness, reliability etc. which matters and which can be ensured through relevant banking technology wherein our banks are lagging behind. This is one of the main contributing factors for high level of consumer dissatisfaction with banks particularly in public sector banks.

The analysis on service quality perceptions between banks and their respective customers reveals that foreign banks are exceeding the perceptions of their customers on tangibility and reliability dimensions of service quality. These banks are not far away from the perceptions of their customers as far as other dimensions of service quality are concerned. In other words foreign banks have correct assessment about the quality of services they are delivering to their customers in comparison to Indian banks. SBI followed by JKB are much below the perceptions of their customers regarding the delivery of quality services. In particular, JKB falls comparatively much below the perceptions of its customers as far as reliability is concerned. The study leads us to the conclusion that all Indian banks, under study, especially JKB followed by SBI and PNB do not have correct assessment of the quality of service they are delivering to their respective customers. Surprisingly, there is no research evidence to support this particular finding of the study.

A significant variation on tangibles followed by responsiveness is reported among the sample organisations. The over all variation in service quality among the sample organisation is 29.62 per cent. Within this variation, the variation on tangibles followed by responsiveness dimensions of service quality is 50.84 and 22.07 per cent respectively, which suggests substantial investment on tangibles as it has direct bearing on responsiveness. This will obviously reduce growing consumer dissatisfaction among Indian banks. This finding supports the earlier findings of the present study on tangibles.

The service quality of foreign banks is considerably high in comparison to public sector banks. Two major reasons can be identified for such high service quality variation: first, foreign banks operate in selected markets and offer selected services; secondly, foreign banks are backed by state of art banking technology which gives them differential/competitive edge in financial services markets. The market share of public sector banks is 81.43 per cent in deposits; 64.50 per cent in advances 90.54 per cent in staff and 89.51% in branch offices (IBA Bulletin special issue March 2002). Processing of volumes of financial services that take place every day, in public sector banks, in absence of relevant banking technology tells upon the delivery of quality services. This fact is evident from high mean differences on tangibility and responsiveness between the two sectors.

The analysis of service quality between public sector and private sector banks leads to conclusion that service quality in private sector banks is relatively better in comparison to public sector banks. However, both sectors are at par on responsiveness dimension of service quality. Service quality of foreign banks is considerably high in comparison to service quality of private sector banks. The operation of foreign banks, in financial services, is selective besides being backed by banking technology gives them a differential edge in delivering quality services. These banks also conduct frequent customer service studies to monitor service standards, which help them to pin point areas of deficiency and thereby corrective measures help them to maintain quality services. This practice is almost absent among Indian banks.

Suggestions and Policy Implications

A number of suggestions have been put forth in connection with delivery of quality service in banks in the relevant chapters. Many of them are of fundamental nature and important and are summarized below along with some other principal recommendations, having broad policy implications.

1. The findings of the study draw attention to the fact that service quality of Indian banks is very poor in comparison to foreign banks particularly on tangibles and responsiveness dimensions of service quality. Our banks are lagging behind on physical facilities, up-to-date equipments, communication material, neatness of employees, busied employees to respond to customers' requests, employees providing prompt service to customers and willingness of employees to help customers'. These findings suggest heavy investment on tangibles particular computer based banking, tele banking, anywhere and anytime banking etc. This will help in delivering quick and accurate services to customers besides reducing the workload of front line staff and thereby providing ways to employees to respond to customer requests. This investment will also take care of convenient banking hours on which our banks' SERVQUAL score is very low in comparison to foreign banks.
2. Mere introduction of banking technology alone will not be sufficient to bring in necessary performance improvement and to get the competitive edge. It is the people who play crucial role in turning the hardware/software and networking tools into a powerful combination to aid the banks in improving their performance. For that purpose proper manpower planning and

training is essential. To exploit the full potential of existing and future technology, it is recommended that banks should create a computer/technology-oriented environment not only in work places but also beyond workplace (at home). Such environments will encourage/motivate the users to broaden or develop their computer related skills, which will ultimately help them to assert themselves vis-à-vis technology. In the same way banks should conduct frequent computer related training programmes to up-grade computer related skills of their employees. The distinguishing aspect of technology area is that, apart from the technical type of training, the technology oriented staff also need training in communication, inter-personal skills, team building and leadership qualities as technical personnel usually lack such skills.

Banks should also conduct frequent training programmes in areas like prompt cash payments and receipts at the counter, efficient pass book and statement service, prompt collection and remittance services, early decisions on credit applications and patient attention to complaints as these areas also have direct bearing on customers service/service quality.

3. 'People' are the most important assets in any organisation particularly in service organisations like banks. A marketing mindset has to be created among the employees, which calls for a flexible approach in case of recruitment and determining of pay scales of employees. A professionalised well-trained and motivated workforce will improve the marketing ability of a bank vis-à-vis its service quality. Since employees play a pivotal role in the

delivery of quality services, therefore, bank management must take care of its employees through proper HRD practices – autonomy an employees is enjoying while performing the job, belongingness he is experiencing with the organisation, recognition he gets from the work he performs and rewards for the good performance he makes.

4. Though technology will play a crucial role in banking, an overwhelming majority of Indian customers may not be touched by this new banking culture, given their obsession towards personalized service. Moreover, there are activities such as account opening and other relationship banking activities for which face to face interaction is all the more important. The bank branch thus remains an important aspect of banking activity and may become a bank's public face. It is, therefore, suggested that banks should make investments in refurbishing their premises as our banks particularly public sector banks have poor SERVQUAL scores on this element of service quality in comparison to private and foreign banks. A well-furnished premise is a must for satisfaction of both employees and customers.

5. The results of the study show that Indian banks are below the expectations of their customers on all dimensions of service quality in comparison to foreign banks which suggests that banks should continually assess and reassess how customers perceive bank services so as to know whether the bank meets or exceeds or is below the expectations of their customers. Such an appraisal is a difficult task because customer service is complex in nature and dynamic in action. What is good service today

may become indifferent service tomorrow and bad service the next day. Frequent customer surveys, therefore, throw light on ratification and refinement, which will go a long way to improve service quality in banks. It is also suggested that some customer's surveys should be conducted through external agencies so that public will repose confidence on the results of the surveys. Opinion polls should be carried out from time to time to understand the perceptions of customers about the bank and other competing banks. It is worth mentioning here that foreign banks organise such surveys quite frequently.

6. A bank of tomorrow has to forget the branch of all trades. Our public sector banks operate in almost all segments, which increase the workload of front line staff thereby leaving them less time to provide individualized or personalized service. This has become one of the major reasons of growing customer dissatisfaction (Bhattacharya, 1989 and Muniraj, 1994). The research findings of present study corroborate the findings of above-mentioned scholars. In the light of these research findings, it is suggested that banks must create branches dedicated to specific lines of business and specific customers. As the number of players is increasing, clients opt for the best service, setting aside the traditional banker customer relationship that covers every service. In other words, in today's liberalized and competitive environment, customers will look for the best bank in each area of business rather than depending upon any one as a one-stop shop. It is, therefore, necessary that banks should specialize in those customer segments where they are strong, which will go a long way in improving

service quality. In the same way banks should create separate branches in each town/local area to take care of government related financial transactions like salaries to government employees, pension holders, sales tax, excise duties, electricity bills, telephone bills etc in each state.

7. Banks must pay attention to potential failure points and service recovery procedures, which become integral to employees training. In other words, it amounts to empowering employees to exercise responsibility, judgement and creativity in responding to customers' problems.

8. In order to overcome growing consumer dissatisfaction it is suggested that banks should make commitment to service quality and the creation of an appropriate culture. The organizational culture may require change, towards employee orientation to the company, and everyone's orientation to the external customer. This change starts at the top; the customer care process must begin with senior management's commitment to employees and customers, ideally with strong and visible leaders.

9. Customer service must match with marketing efforts otherwise a customer would remain a dissatisfied soul and all marketing efforts will go down the drain. The process of fulfilling customer needs, therefore, requires tailoring bank services to what customer wants, rather than making them to accept whatever banks can conveniently provide. The need and expectations of the customer changes from time to time and as such innovating of new services and refinement of existing services is imperative. Today customers are exposed to the

standards of international banking and expect same range of service quality from Indian banks. If Indian banks fail to regulate their financial services to that of foreign banks, time is not far away when they will loose substantial market share to foreign banks.

10. Lastly, managing the perceived service quality means that the firm has to match the expected service and the perceived service to each other so that consumer satisfaction is achieved. In order to keep the gap between the expected service and the perceived service as small as possible it is important that the promises about how the service will perform, given by traditional marketing activities, and communicated by word of mouth, must not be unrealistic when compared to the service the customers eventually will perceive.

The study has identified some factors which have a direct bearing on consumer dissatisfaction in banks particularly in public sector banks. The investigator has reasons to believe that the conclusions of the study, along with the suggestions, if rightly perceived and properly implemented will certainly go a long way in improving service quality in banks. Since consumer behavior is dynamic in nature and consumer expectations change continuously, as the level of income, education or socio-economic environment changes, there is always need for research and in-depth study to bring out, from time to time, the factors responsible for consumer satisfaction/dissatisfaction in banks. The present study has brought out some research gaps, which have a strong bearing on service quality vis-à-vis performance in banks. It is, therefore, suggested that more detailed investigations into such vital issues need to be taken up by separate comparative and contextual studies.

Appendices

APPENDIX-I

QUESTIONNAIRE FOR BANK CUSTOMERS

Instructions

Based on your experience as a bank customer, please think about the kind of bank that would deliver excellent quality service. Think about the kind of a bank with which you would be pleased to do business. Please show the extent to which you think such a bank would possess the features described by each statement. If you feel a feature is not at all essential for excellent banks such as the one you have in mind, circle number 1. If you feel a feature is absolutely essential for excellent banks, circle 7. If your feelings are less strong, circle one of the numbers in the middle. There is no right or wrong answers – all I am interested is a number that truly reflects your feelings regarding banks that would deliver excellent quality service.

	Strongly Disagree	Disagree	Slightly Disagree	Neither Agree nor Disagree	Slightly Agree	Agree	Strongly Agree
1. Excellent banks will have modern looking equipment.	1	2	3	4	5	6	7
2. The physical facilities at excellent banks will be visually appealing.	1	2	3	4	5	6	7
3. Employees at excellent banks will be neat appearing.	1	2	3	4	5	6	7
4. Materials associated with the service (such as pamhlets or statements) will be visually appealing in an excellent bank.	1	2	3	4	5	6	7
5. When excellent bank promise to do something by a certain time, they will do so.	1	2	3	4	5	6	7
6. When a customer has a problem, excellent banks will show a sincere interest in solving it.	1	2	3	4	5	6	7
7. Excellent banks will perform the service right the first time.	1	2	3	4	5	6	7
8. Excellent banks will provide their services at the time they promise to do so.	1	2	3	4	5	6	7
9. Excellent banks will insist on error-free records.	1	2	3	4	5	6	7
10. Employees in excellent banks will tell customers exactly when services will be performed.	1	2	3	4	5	6	7
11. Employees in excellent banks will give prompt service to customers.	1	2	3	4	5	6	7
12. Employees in excellent banks will always be willing to help customers..	1	2	3	4	5	6	7
13. Employees in excellent banks	1	2	3	4	5	6	7

	will never be too busy to respond to customer's requests.							
14.	The behaviour of employees in excellent banks will instill confidence in customers.	1	2	3	4	5	6	7
15.	Customers of excellent banks will feel safe in their transactions.	1	2	3	4	5	6	7
16.	Employees in excellent banks will be consistently courteous with customers.	1	2	3	4	5	6	7
17.	Employees in excellent banks will have the knowledge to answer customers' questions.	1	2	3	4	5	6	7
18.	Excellent banks will give customers individual attention.	1	2	3	4	5	6	7
19.	Excellent banks will have operating hours convenient to all their customers.	1	2	3	4	5	6	7
20.	Excellent banks will have employees who give customers personal attention.	1	2	3	4	5	6	7
21.	Excellent banks will have the customer's best interest at heart.	1	2	3	4	5	6	7
22.	The employees of excellent banks will understand the specific needs of their customers.	1	2	3	4	5	6	7

Instructions

Listed below are five features pertaining to banks and the services they offer. I would like to know how much important each of these features is to you when you evaluate a bank's quality of service. Please rank them from 1 to 5 in order of their importance. Rank 1 is very important and rank 5 is least important.

		Rank
1.	The appearance of the banksphysical facilities, equipment, personnel, and communication materials.	__________

2. The banks ability to perform the promised service dependably and accurately. __________
3. The banks willingness to help customers and provide prompt service. __________
4. The knowledge and courtesy of the banks employees and their ability to convey trust and confidence. __________
5. The caring, individualized attention the bank provides its customer. __________

Instructions

The following set of statements relates to your feelings about your bank. For each statement, please show the extent to which you believe your bank has the feature described by the statement. Once again, circling 1 means that you strongly disagree that your bank has that feature, and circling 7 means that you strongly agree. You may circle any of the numbers in the middle that show how strong your feelings are. There is no right or wrong answers – all I am interested in is a number that best shows your perceptions about your bank.

	Strongly Disagree	Disagree	Slightly Disagree	Neither Agree nor Disagree	Slightly Agree	Agree	Strongly Agree
1. Your bank has modern–looking equipment.	1	2	3	4	5	6	7
2. Your bank's physical facilities are visually appealing.	1	2	3	4	5	6	7
3. Your banks employees are neat appearing.	1	2	3	4	5	6	7
4. Materials associated with the service (such as pamphlets or statement) are visually appealing at your bank.	1	2	3	4	5	6	7
5. When your bank promises to do something by a certain time, it does so	1	2	3	4	5	6	7
6. When you have a problem,	1	2	3	4	5	6	7

your bank shows a sincere interest in solving it.							
7. Your bank performs its services at the time it promises to do so.	1	2	3	4	5	6	7
8. Your bank performs the service right the first time.	1	2	3	4	5	6	7
9. Your bank insists on error-free records.	1	2	3	4	5	6	7
10. Employees in your bank tell you exactly when services will be performed.	1	2	3	4	5	6	7
11. Employees in your bank give you prompt service.	1	2	3	4	5	6	7
12. Employees in your bank are always willing to help you.	1	2	3	4	5	6	7
13. Employees in your bank are never too busy to respond to your requests.	1	2	3	4	5	6	7
14. The behaviour of employees in your bank instills confidence in you.	1	2	3	4	5	6	7
15. You feel safe in your transactions with your bank.	1	2	3	4	5	6	7
16. Employees in your bank are consistently courteous with you.	1	2	3	4	5	6	7
17. Employees in your bank have the knowledge to answer your questions.	1	2	3	4	5	6	7
18. Your bank gives you individual attention.	1	2	3	4	5	6	7
19. Your bank has operating hours convenient to all customers.	1	2	3	4	5	6	7
20. Your bank has employees who give you personal attention.	1	2	3	4	5	6	7
21. Your bank has your best interests at heart.	1	2	3	4	5	6	7
22. Employees of your bank understand your specific needs.	1	2	3	4	5	6	7

DEMOGRAPHIC DATA

Instructions: Please mark cross (´) in the space/s relevant to you.

1. Age in years : 20 – 35
   35 – 50
   Above 50
2. Gender : a) Male——— b) Female———
3. Education : Bachelors Degree/Diploma ————
   Post-graduate/Diploma ————
   Professional/Technical Qualification—
   Any Other, please mention ———
4. Level of Income : 5000 – 15000 p.m.
   15000 – 25000 p.m.
   25000 – 35000 p.m.
   Above 35000 p.m.
5. Location of Bank : J&K State___Kashmir/Jammu___
   Punjab————————————
   Delhi————————————
6. Residence : _________________________
   ____
   ____
7. Profession : _________________________
8. Your Bank : State Bank of India ————
   Punjab National Bank ————
   J&K Bank ————————
   City Bank ————————
   Standard Chartered Grindlay's Bank —
   Department of Commerce————
   University of Kashmir, Srinagar.———

APPENDIX-II

QUESTIONNAIRE FOR BANK OFFICIALS

Instructions

The following set of statements relates to the perceptions held by your customers about your bank. For each statement, please show the extent to which you believe your bank has the feature described by the statement as known to and perceived by you. If you feel a feature is not at all essential for your bank as perceived by your customers, circle number1 and if you feel a feature is absolutely essential, circle number 7. If your feelings are less strong, circle one of the numbers in the middle. There is no right or wrong answers _____ all I am interested is a number that truly reflects your feelings about your customers of your bank.

	Strongly Disagree	Disagree	Slightly Disagree	Neither Agree nor Disagree	Slightly Agree	Agree	Strongly Agree
1. Excellent banks will have modern looking equipment.	1	2	3	4	5	6	7
2. The physical facilities at excellent banks will be visually appealing.	1	2	3	4	5	6	7
3. Employees at excellent banks will be neat appearing.	1	2	3	4	5	6	7
4. Materials associated with the service (such as pamhlets or statements) will be visually appealing in an excellent bank.	1	2	3	4	5	6	7
5. When excellent bank promise to do something by a certain time, they will do so.	1	2	3	4	5	6	7
6. When a customer has a problem, excellent banks will show a sincere interest in solving it.	1	2	3	4	5	6	7
7. Excellent banks will perform the service right the first time.	1	2	3	4	5	6	7
8. Excellent banks will provide their services at the time they promise to do so.	1	2	3	4	5	6	7
9. Excellent banks will insist on error-free records.	1	2	3	4	5	6	7
10. Employees in excellent banks will tell customers exactly when services will be performed.	1	2	3	4	5	6	7
11. Employees in excellent banks will give prompt service to customers.	1	2	3	4	5	6	7
12. Employees in excellent banks will always be willing to help customers.	1	2	3	4	5	6	7

13. Employees in excellent banks will never be too busy to respond to customer's requests.	1	2	3	4	5	6	7
14. The behaviour of employees in excellent banks will instill confidence in customers.	1	2	3	4	5	6	7
15. Customers of excellent banks will feel safe in their transactions.	1	2	3	4	5	6	7
16. Employees in excellent banks will be consistently courteous with customers.	1	2	3	4	5	6	7
17. Employees in excellent banks will have the knowledge to answer customers' questions.	1	2	3	4	5	6	7
18. Excellent banks will give customers individual attention.	1	2	3	4	5	6	7
19. Excellent banks will have operating hours convenient to all their customers.	1	2	3	4	5	6	7
20. Excellent banks will have employees who give customers personal attention.	1	2	3	4	5	6	7
21. Excellent banks will have the customer's best interest at heart.	1	2	3	4	5	6	7
22. The employees of excellent banks will understand the specific needs of their customers.	1	2	3	4	5	6	7

Instructions

Listed below are five features pertaining to banks and the services they offer. I would like to know how much important each of these features is to you when you evaluate a banks quality of service. Please rank them from 1 – 5 in order of their importance. Rank 1 is very important and rank 5 is least important.

	Rank
1. The appearance of the banksphysical facilities, equipment, personnel, and communication materials.	______
2. The banks ability to perform the promised service dependably and accurately.	______
3. The banks willingness to help customers and provide prompt service.	______
4. The knowledge and courtesy of the banks employees and their ability to convey trust and confidence.	______
5. The caring, individualized attention the bank provides its customer.	______

PERSONAL DATA

Instructions: Please mark cross (´) in the space/s relevant to you.

1. Age in years	:	20 – 35
		35 – 50
		Above 50
2. Gender	:	a) Male——— b) Female———
3. Education	:	Bachelors Degree/Diploma ———
		Post-graduate/Diploma ———
		Professional/Technical Qualification—
		Any Other, please mention ———
4. Scale	:	Ist———
		IInd———
		IIIrd———
		IVth———
		Vth———
		VIth———
5. Location of Bank	:	J&K State____Kashmir/Jammu____
		Punjab———
		Delhi———
		______

6. Residence : ______________________________

____

____

7. Bank you are serving : State Bank of India ______________

Punjab National Bank ______________

J&K Bank ______________

City Bank ______________

Standard Chartered Grindlay's Bank —

Select Bibliography

Aggrawal, M. (1998) "Rising Productivity in a Service Organisation: The Role of Pace & Customer Participation", *Paradigm,* Vol. 1, No. 2, January, pp. 70-77.

Aishah, S. (1997) "The Key to Success", *Chartered Financial Analyst,* June, p. 70.

Ajit, S. (1986) "Training for Bank Marketing", Financial Express, Bombay, December 31, p. 6

Albrecht, K. and Zemke, R. (1985) "Service America: Doing Business in the New York" in Lewis Barbara (1991) "Service Quality: An International Comparison of Bank Customers Expectations and Perceptions", *Journal of Marketing Management,* Vol. 7, pp. 47-62.

Ammayya, T. (1996) "Developing Competitive Advantage Through Absorption of Technology in Knowledge, Skills and Attitudes of People", *IBA Bulletin,* Vol. XVIII, No. 12, October-December, pp. 38-42.

Anderson, C. and Zeithaml, C.P. (1984) "Stage of Product Life Cycle, Business Strategy, and Business Performance", *Academy of Management Journal,* Vol. 27, March, pp. 5-24

Andrine, P. (1995), *The Essence of Services Marketing,* Prentice Hall of India, New Delhi, 224-226.

Aul, G.D. (1994) "Problems and Challenges in Marketing of

Bank Services", in Bidhi, C. (Ed.), (1994) *Marketing of Services*, Rawat Publications, New Delhi, p. 43.

Babakus, E and Boller, G.W. (1992) "An Empirical Assessment of the SERVQUAL Scale", *Journal of Business Research*, Vol. 24, May, pp. 253-268.

Babakus, E. and Boller, C.W. (1991), "An Empirical Assessment of The SERQUAL Scale", *Journal of Business Research*, Vol. 24, pp. 253-268.

Bapat, S. G. (1980) "Customer Service in Urban Cooperative Banks", *The Journal of Indian Institute of Bankers*, Vol. 51, No. 2, pp. 13,71-80.

Barnes, J, G (1997) "Closeness, Strength, and Satisfaction: Examining the Nature of Relationships Between Providers of Financial Service and Their Retail Customers", *Psychology and Marketing*, Vol. 14, No. 8, pp. 765-790.

Bateson, J. E.G. (1995) *Managing Service Marketing, Text and Readings*, The Dryden Press, New York, pp. .9-10, 457, 558-579.

Bateson, J.E.G. (1979) "Why are Need Service Marketing" in Zeithaml V.A., Panasuraman A and Berry L. (1985), Problems and Strategies in Service Marketing, *Journal of Marketing*, Vol. 49. No. 2, p. 33.

Bateson, J.E.G. (1977) "Do We Need Services Marketing", in Zeihaml, V.A. (1985) "Problems and Strategies in Services Marketing", *Journal of Marketing*, Vol. 49, Spring, pp. 33-46.

Bazzel, R.D. and Wiersema, F.D. (1981) "Successful Share Building Strategies," *Harvard Business Review*, January – February, p. 135.

Benjamen, S. and Bowen, D.E. (1993) "The Service Organisation: Human Resource Management is Crucial", *Organizational Dynamics*, Spring, pp. 39-52.

Benjamin, S. (1980) "The Service Organisation: Climate is Crucial", *Organizational Dynamics*, Autumn, pp. 52-65.

Berry, L. L., Parasuraman, A. and Zeithaml, V.A. (1994) "Improving Service Quality in America – Lessons Learned," *Academy of Management Executive*, Vol. 8, No. 2, pp. 32-52.

Berry, L.L. (1980) "Services Marketing is Different," *Business* Vol. 30, (May-June), pp. 8-30

Berry, L.L. and Parasuraman, A. (1991) *Marketing Services: Competing Through Quality*, Maxwell Macmillan International, New York, pp. 175-203.

Berry, L.L., Bennett, D.R. and Brown C.W. (1989) "Service Quality: A Profit Strategy for Financial Institutions", *Homewood Illinois, Dow Jones Irwin;* in Lewis Barbara (1991) "Service Quality: An International Comparison of Bank Customers Expectations and Perceptions", *Journal of Marketing Management*, Vol. 7, pp. 47-62.

Bessom, R.M. (1973) "Unique Aspects of Marketing of Services," *Arizona Business Bulletin*, November, p. 9.

Bhattacharaya, B.N. and Ghose, B.K. (1989) "Marketing of Banking Services in the 90s, Problems and Perspectives", *Economic and Political Weekly*, February 25, Vol. 24, No. 8.

Bhide, M.G. (1997) "Information Technology in Banks," *IBA Bulletin*, Vol. 68, No. 4, October-December, pp. 149-152.

Bitner, M.J., Booms B.H. and Tetreault M.S. (1990), "The Service Encounter: Diagnosing Favorable and

Unfavorable Incidents", *Journal of Marketing,* January Vol. 55, pp. 71-84.

Blois, K.J. (1974) "The Marketing of Services", *European Journal of Marketing,* summer, p. 157.

Bolton, R.N. and Drew, J.H. (1991a), "A Longitudinal Analysis of the Impact of Service Changes on Consumer Attitudes", *Journal of Marketing,* Vol. 55, January, pp. 1-9.

Bolton, R.N. and Drew J.H. (1991b), "A Multistage Model of Customer's Assessment of Service Quality and Value", *Journal of Consumer Research,* Vol. 17, No. 4, pp. 375-384.

Bansal, L. K. (1984) "Marketing of Bank Services at Grossroot Level", in Bidhi, C. (1994) (Ed.), *Marketing of Services* Rawat Publications, New Delhi, p. 73.

Booms, B.H. and Bitnar, M.J. (1981) "Marketing Strategies and Organisation Structures for Services Firms", in Marketing of Services, Donnelly, S.H. and George, W.R. (eds.), *American Marketing Association,* Chicago, Ill., pp. 47-51.

Booms, B.H. and Bitner M.J. (1981) "Marketing Strategies and Organisation Structures for Services Firms", in Zeithaml V.A. Panasuraman A, and Berry L.L (1985) "Problems and Strategies in Service Marketing", *Journal of Marketing,* Vol. 49, No. 2 pp. 33-46.

Brahmanandan, G.N. and Narayana, M.S. (1990) "A Study on Customer Service in Commercial Banks", *Indian Journal of Marketing,* Vol. 20, No. 5, January, pp. 7-8 and 16.

Brown, S.W. and Swartz, T.A. (1989), "A Gap Analysis of Professional Service Quality", *Journal of Marketing,* Vol. 49, April, pp. 92-100.

Buzzell, R.D. and Gale, B.T. (1987) "The PIMS Principles – Linking Strategy to Performance" in Christopher H Lovelock (1996) *Service Marketing*, 3rd Ed., Prentice Hall, New Jersey, p. 462.

Buzzell, R.D. and Wiersema, F.D (1981), :Successful Share-building Strategies", *Harvard Business Review*, January-February p. 135.

Carman, J.M. (1990) "Consumer Perceptions of Service Quality" An Assessment of the SERVQUAL Dimensions", *Journal of Retailing*, Vol. 66, Spring, pp. 33-56.

Carman, J.M. and Langeard. E. (1980) "Growth Strategies of Service Firms", *Strategic Management Journal*, Vol. 1, (January – March) pp. 7-22.

Carson, D. and Gilmore, A. (1989) "Customer Care: The Neglected Domain", *Irish Marketing Review*, Vol. 4, No. 3, pp. 49-61.

Chaudhari, P. R. (1981) "Customer Service in Banks", *Management Accountant*, Vol. 16, No. 3, p. 121.

Chidambaram, R.M. (1996) "Total Quality Management in Bank's Lending", *State Bank of India, Monthly Review*, Vol. 35, No. 2, March, pp. 103-108.

Chidambaram, R.M. and Alamelu, K.M.S. (1996) "Services Marketing: Challenges and Strategies", *State Bank of India Monthly Review*, Vol. 35, No. 6, June, pp. 303-308.

Chidanbaram, R.M. (1996) "Services Marketing – Challenges and Strategies", *State Bank of India, Monthly Review*, Vol. 35, No. 6, June, pp. 303-308.

Cronin, J.J. and Taylor, S.A. (1992) "Measuring Service Quality: A Re-examination and Extension", *Journal of Marketing*, Vol. 56, July, pp. 55-68.

Crosby, P. B. (1979), *Quality is Free,* McGraw Hill, New York.

Devlin, S.J. and Dong, H.K. (1996) "Service Quality from Customers Perspective," *Marketing Research,* Vol. 6, No. 1, pp. 5-13.

Fick, G.R. and Ritchie, J.R.B. (1991), "Measuring Service Quality in the Travel and Tourism Industry", *Journal of Travel Research,* Vol. 30, No. 3, pp. 2-9.

Gale, B.T. (1994) "Managing Customer Value" in Christopher H Lovelock (1996) *Service Markeinng,* 3rd Prentice Hall, New Jersey, p. 462.

Ganguly, A.K. (1983) "Growth Sans Service", *The Economic Times,* October 15, p. 5.

Garvin, D.A. (1983) "Quality on the Line" *Harvard Business Review,* Vol. 61, No. 5, Sept. – October, pp. 65-73.

Garvin, D.A. (1988) *Managing Quality,* Free Press, New York, pp. 40-41.

Ghose, B.K. (1982) "Productivity in Banks", *State Bank of India Monthly Review,* August, p. 304.

Ghose, B.K. (1987) "Bank Nationalisation: Promise and Performance", *The Journal of Indian Institute of Bankers,* July-September, p. 126.

Gilmore, A. and Carson, D. (1993) "Quality Improvement in a Services Marketing Context", *Journal of Services Marketing,* Vol. 7, No. 3. pp. 6-21, 59-71.

Girish, V. and Preetha, S. (1997) "Technology in Banks – A Global Perspective", *IBA Bulletin,* Vol. 68, No. 4, October-December, pp. 183-189.

Godse, V.T. (1997) "Banking Technology: Challenges Ahead for Banks", *IBA Bulletin,* Vol. 68, No. 4, October-December, pp. 180-182.

Goodman, J.A., Marra, T. and Brigham L. (1986) "Customer Service: Costly Nuisance or Low Cost Profit Strategy", *Journal of Retail Banking,* Vol. 8. No. 3, pp. 7-16.

Goyal, R. P. (1983) "Improving Quality of Banking Service", *Commerce,* (Banking Supplement) July 30th, p. 3.

Gronroos, C. (1982), "Strategic Management and Marketing in the Services Sector" in Parasuraman A., Zeithaml V.A and Berry L.L (1985) "A Conceptual Model of Service Quality and its Implications for Future Research", *Journal of Marketing,* Fall Vol. , 49, pp. 41-50.

Gronroos, C. (1984) "A Service Quality Model and its Marketing Implications", *European Journal of Marketing,* Vol. , 18, No. 4, pp. 36-50

Gronroos, C. (1990) *Service Management – And Marketing,* Massachusetts -Lexington Books, p. 27.

Gronross, C. (1978) "A Service Oriented Approach to Marketing of Services", *European Journal of Marketing,* Vol. 12, No. 8, pp. 588-601.

Gronross, C. (1979) "An Applied Theory for Marketing Industrial Services", *Industrial Marketing Management,* Vol. 8, January, pp. 45-50.

Gronross, C. (1982), "Strategic Management and Marketing in the Service Sector", Hilsinki, Finland, Swedish School of Economics and Business Administration.

Gronross, C. (1983) "Strategic Management and Marketing in the Service Sector" in Lovelock, C.H. (1996) *Service Marketing,* Prentice Hall, New Jersey, p. 85.

Gronross, C. (1988) "Service Quality: The Sixth Criteria of Good Perceived Service Quality", *Review of Business,* Vol. 9, No. 3, (Winter), pp. 10-13.

Grossman, R.P. (1998) "Developing and Managing Effective Consumer Relations", *Journal of Product and Brand Management*, Vol. 7, No. 1, pp. 27-40.

Gummenson, E. (1998) "Implementation Requires a Relationship Marketing Paradigm", *Journal of the Academy of Marketing Science*, Vol. 26, No. 3, pp. 242-249.

Gummensson, E. and Gronroos, C. (1987) "Quality of Products and Services: A Tentative Synthesis Between Two Models", Research Report, Services Research Centre, University of Karlstad, Sweden.

Gummerson, E. (1987) "Lip Services – A Neglected Area in Services Marketing", *Journal of Services Marketing*, No. 1, p. 22.

Gupta, R.K. and Bansal, L.K. (1994) "Bank Services and Marketing Approach", in Bidhi, C. (1994) (Ed.) *Marketing of Services*, Rawat Publications, New Delhi, pp. 74-81.

Gurdeep, S. (1994) "Marketing of Services in Banking Sector: Challenges Ahead", in Bidhi, C. (1994) (Ed.), *Marketing of Services*, Rawat Publications, New Delhi, pp. 82-90.

Harsh, V.V. (1993) *Marketing of Services*, Global Business Press, New Delhi, pp. 100-121.

Hart, C.W. (1988) "The Power of Unconditional Service Guarantee", *Harvard Business Review*, July-August, pp. 54-62.

Hostage, G.M. (1975) "Quality Control in a Service Business", *Harvard Business Review*, July – August, pp. 98-106.

Ingram, T. and Laforge, R. (1989) *Sales Management: Analysis and Decision Making*, The Dryden Press, Florida, p. 70.

Johns, N. (1993), "Quality Management in the Hospitality

Industry", *International Journal of Contemporary Hospitality Management*, Vol. 5, No. 1, pp. 10-15.

Karandikar, S.K. (1999) "Total Bank Automation for Nationalised Banks", *IBA Bulletin*, Vol. XXI, No. 2, February, pp. 29-30.

Kotlar, P. (1999) *Marketing Management: The Millennium Edition*, Prentice Hall of India, New Delhi, pp. 50-58.

Kotlar, P. and Bloom P. N. (1984) *Marketing Professional Services*, Prentice Hall , New Jersey, p. 174.

Kotler, P. (1980) *Marketing Management: Analysis, Planning and Control*, Prentice Hall of India, New Delhi, p. 12.

Kotler, P. (1999) *Marketing Management*, Prentice Hall of India, New Delhi, pp. 434-444.

Kotler, P. and Armstrong, G. (1987) *Marketing: An Introduction*, Prentice Hall, Englewood Cliffs, New Jersey, p. 8.

Langeard, E., Beatson J.E.G. and Lovelock C.H. (1981), *Service Marketing: New Insight from Consumer and Managers*, Marketing Service Institute, Cambridge.

Laxaman, G. (1983), "Customer Service in Banks", *The Economic Times*, October 15, p. 6.

Lehtinen, U. and Lehtinan, J.R. (1982) "Service Quality: A Study of Quality Dimensions", *Working Paper*, Service Management Institute, Helsinki, Finland.

Lehtinen, U. and Lehtinen, J.R. (1991) "Two Approaches to Service Quality Dimensions", *The Service Industries Journal*, Vol. 11, No. 3, pp. 287-303.

Leonard, F.S. and Sasser, E.W. (1982), "The Incline of Quality", *Harvard Business Review*, September-October; Vol. 60; No. 5; pp. 163-171.

Levitt, T. (1981) "Marketing Intangible Products and Product Intangibles", *Harvard Business Review,* May – June, pp. 94-102.

Lewis, B. (1991), "Service Quality: An International Comparison of Bank Customers Expectations and Perceptions", *Journal of Marketing Management,* Vol. 7, pp. 47-62.

Lewis, B.R. (1993) "Service Quality Measurement", *Marketing Intelligence and Planning,* Vol. 11, No. 4, pp. 4-12.

Lewis, B.R. and Mitchell, V.W. (1990), "Defining and Measuring the Quality of Customer Service", *Marketing Intelligence and Planning,* Vol. 8, No. 6, pp. 11-18.

Lewis, R.C. (1987), "The Measurement of Gaps in the Quality of Hotel Service", *International Journal of Hospitality Management,* Vol. 6, No. 2, pp. 83-91.

Lewis, R.C. and Booms, B.H. (1983) "The Marketing Aspect of Service Quality" in Lewis, B.R. (1981) Service Quality: An International Comparison of Bank Customers Expectations and Perceptions", *Journal of Marketing Management,* Vol. 7, pp. 47-62.

Lewis, R.C. and Booms, B.H. (1983) "The Marketing Aspect of Service Quality" in Emerging Perspectives on Services Marketing; L. Berry, G. Shostack, and G. Upah (Eds)., *American Marketing Association,* Chicago, pp. 99-102.

Linjander, V. and Strandrik, T. (1994), "The Nature of Relationship Quality" in Carson, D. and. Gilmore, A. (1996) (Eds.) *Services Marketing, Text and Readings,* Mercury Publications Ltd. Dublin, pp. 41-49, 255-277

Lovelock, C.H. (1981) "Why Marketing Management Needs to be Different for Services", in Zeithaml, V. A., et.al. (1985) *Problems and Strategies in Services Marketing, Journal of Marketing,* Vol. 49, Spring (1985), pp. 33-46.

Lovelock, C.H. (1996), *Service Marketing,* Prentice Hall of India Pvt. Ltd., New Delhi, p. 316.

Madhukar, R.K. (1990), *Dynamics of Bank Marketing,* Shri Sudhindra Publishing House, I/E, Banglore, p. 81.

Marshall, C.E. (1985) "Can we Be Consumer-Oriented in a Changing Financial Service World", *The Journal of Consumer Marketing,* Vol. 2, No. 4, Fall pp. 37-43.

Middleton, P. (1994) "Towards Globalisation and International Competitiveness", *IBA Bulletin,* Vol. XVI, No. 11, November, pp. 8-11.

Mohan, R.M. (1983) "Banking Industry: Productivity and Personnel Policy", *The Economic Times,* June 29th.

Muniraj, R. (1994) "Strategies to Improve Customer Service in Banks", *The Banker,* June, pp. 31-34.

Nageswar, R. (1987) "Customer Service in Banks Must Improve", *Yojana,* Vol. 31, No. 13, July 16-31, pp. 20-31.

Nageswar, R. and Pramod, P. (1990) "customer Services and Banks", *Yojana,* Vol. 34, No. 13, July 16-13, pp. 15-22.

Naidu, C.A.S. (1997) "Information Technology and Organisational Effectiveness", *IBA Bulletin,* Vol. 68, No. 4, October-December, pp. 168-173.

Panasuraman, A., Zeithaml V.A. and Berry. L.L. (1988), "SERVQUAL: A Multiple Scale for Measuring Consumer Perceptions of service Quality", *Journal of Retailing,* Vol. 64, No. 1, Spring, pp. 12-40.

Panasuraman, A.., Zeithaml V.A. and Berry. L.L. (1985), "A Conceptual Model of Service Quality and Its Implications for Future Research", *Journal of Marketing,* Vol. 49, Fall, pp. 41-50.

Parasuraman, A., Berry, L. and Zeithaml, V.A. (1990), "Guidelines for Conducting Service Quality Research", *Marketing Research* (December), 34-44.

Parasuraman, A., Berry, L. and Zeithaml, V.A. (1991) "Perceived Service Quality as a Customer- Based Performance Measure: An Empirical Examination of Organizational Barriers Using an Extended Service Quality Model", *Human Resource Management*, Vo. 30, No. 3, pp. 335-364.

Parasuraman, A., Berry, L.L. and Zeithaml, V. A. (1991), "Undertaking Customer Expectations of Service", *Sloan Management Review*, Spring, p. 44.

Parasuraman, A., Berry, L.L., and Zeithaml, V.A. (1991) "Refinement and Reassessment of the SERVQUAL Scale", *Journal of Retailing*, Vol. 67, Winter, pp. 420-450.

Parasuraman, A., Zeithaml, V.A. and Barry, L.L. (1994), "Reassessment of Expectations as a Comparison Standard in Measuring Service Quality: Implications from Further Research", *Journal of Marketing*, Vol. 58, No. 1. pp. 111-124.

Parthasarathi, R. (1995) "Strategic Planning in the Emerging Environment", *IBA Bulletin*, Vol. XVII, No. 5, May pp. 15-17.

Phillips, C.W., Chang, D.R. and Buzzel, D. (1983) "Product Quality, Cost Position and Business Performance: A test of some key hypothesis", *Journal of Marketing*, Vol. 47(Spring) 26-43.

Pitt, L.F., Oosthuizen, P. and Morris, M.H. (1992), "Service Quality in a High-Tech Industrial Market: An Application of SERVQUAL", *American Marketing Association Proceedings*, Summer, Chicago.

Prahlad, S. (2001) "The World Trade Organization and the Role of Banks", *The Journal of the Indian Institute of Bankers*, Vol. 72, No. 1, January-March, pp. 20-32.

Radhakrishnan and Baber, P. (1984) "Mechanisation: Better Cheque Handling", *The Economic Times*, October 15, p. 5.

Rajan, N.N. (1992) "Marketing of Bank Services", *The Banker*, Vol. 39, No. 9, November, p. 20.

Ramachandra, R.B. (1992) "Where the Bankers are not Market-Friendly", *The Banker*, 39(9):26-28.

Ramchandra, R. (1983) "Bank Employees Agitations", *The Hindu*, April 5.

Rao, K.V. (1984) "Quality Circles in Banks", *The Hindu*, February 20th.

Rayudu, C.S. (1990) "Banks Social Marketing and Market Segmentation", *Indian Journal of Marketing*, Vol. 20, No. 9-12, May-August, pp. 3-6 and 20.

Regan, W.J. (1963) "The Services Revolution", *Journal of Marketing*, July, p. 57.

Reichheld, F.F. and Sasser, E.W. (1990) "Zero Defections: Quality Comes to Service", *Harvard Business Review*, September – October, pp. 105-111.

Robert, J.C. (1964) "The Case for Redefining Services", *Journal of Marketing*, Vol. , 28, January.

Ross, J.E. and Shetty, Y.K. (1985), "Making Quality a Fundamental Part of Strategy", in Lewis B. (1991) "Service Quality: An International Comparison of Bank Customers Expectations and Perceptions", *Journal of Marketing Management*, Vol. 7, pp. 47-62.

Saleh, F. and Ryan, C. (1991), "Analysing Service Quality in the Hospitality Industry Using the SERVQUAL Model", *Service Industries Journal,* Vol. 11, No. 3, pp. 324-343.

Salma, A. (1998) "Technological reforms in the Banking Sector", *NMIMS Management Review,* Vol. X, No. 1, pp. 21-27.

Saraf, W.S., (1997) "Banking Technology: Agenda Ahead", IBA Bulletin, Vol. 68, No. 4, October-December, pp. 153-155.

Sasser, W.E., Olsen, R.P., and Wyckoff D.D (1978) "Understanding Service Operations", in *Management of Service Operations,* Boston: Allyn and Bacon.

Satish, G.H. and Nandakumar, M. (1995) "Customer Relations: Need for Comprehensive Approach", *Indian Journal of Marketing,* Vol. 24, No. 5, May, pp. 25-27.

Saxena, K.K. (1985) 'Evolution of Bank Marketing in India', *State Bank of India, Monthly Review,* February.

Saxena, K.K. (1988) "Bank Marketing: Concepts and Applications", Skylark Publications, New Delhi, p. 10, 147-166.

Schoeffler, S., Buzzell, R.D. and Heany, D.E. (1974), "Impact of Strategic Planning on Profit Performance", *Harvard Business Review,* March-April, p. 137.

Screenivasan, P.B. (1987) "Marketing Approach to Banking Services", *Journal of Indian Institute of Bankers,* Vol. 58, No. 3, p. 129.

Sesha Sai, P.V. (1999) "Customer Service – Some HRD Interventions", *IBA Bulletin,* Vol. XXI, No. 2, February, pp. 11-16.

Shah, S.G. (1982) "Training for Customer Service", *Commerce,* March 13th, p. 471.

Shankar, C. (1995) "As the Money Flies", Chartered Financial Analyst, October, p. 31.

Shankar, R. (1999), *Services Marketing: The Indian Experience,* South Asia Publications, New Delhi, p. 6.

Sheikh, M.N. (1996) "Profasionalising Service Marketing", *Indian Journal of Marketing,* Vol. XXV, No. 5-6; May-June, pp. 17-20.

Smith, A.M. (1992), "The Consumer's Evaluation of Service Quality: Some Methodological Issues" in Glynn, W.J. and Barnes, J.G. (1995) (Eds.), *Understanding Services Management,* John Willey & Sons, New York, pp. 57-88.

Smith, S. (1987) "How to Quantify Quality", *Management Today,* October, pp. 86-94.

Sreedhar, G. (1991) "Marketing Style of Indian Banks", *The Banker,* Vol. 37, No. 12, February, p. 29.

Srivastava, A.K. (1994) "Customer Service in Banks: Need for a Marketing Approach" in Bidhi, C. (1994), *Marketing of Services,* Rawat Publications, New Delhi, pp. 25-38.

Srivastava, T. N. (1997) "Banking Technology: Educational/ Training Challenges", *IBA Bulletin,* Vol. 68, No. 4, October-December, pp. 174-179.

Stanton, W.J. (1974) "Fundamentals of Marketing. McGraw-Hill, Tokyo, p. 545.

Sundaram, S. (1984) "Customer Service in Banks at Crossroads", *The Journal of the Indian Institute of Bankers,* Vol. 55, No. 4, pp. 217-223.

Susan, J. D. and Dong, H.K. (1994) "Service Quality from Customer's Perspective", *Marketing Research,* Vol. , 6, No. 1, pp. 5-13.

Takeuchi, H. and Quelch, J.A. (1983), "Quality is more than Making a Good Product", *Harvard Business Review;* July-Aug; pp. 139-145.

Uttal, B. (1987) "Companies that Serve Yon Best", *Fortune,* December 2nd; pp98-101.

Vijay, L. M., (1991) "Bank Marketing: A Long Way To Go", *Quarterly Economic Report of the Institute of Public Opinion,* Vol. 34, No. 2, July-September, pp. 43-50.

Woodruffe, H. (1998) *Services Marketing* Macmillan India Ltd., New Delhi, pp. 19,31, 95-105.

Young, C., Cunningham, L. and Lee, M. (1994) "Accessing Service Quality as an Effective Management Tool: The Case of Airline Industry", *Journal of Marketing: Theory and Practice,* Spring, pp. 76-95.

Zeithamal, V.A. and Bitner, M.J. (1996), *Services Marketing: Integrating Customer Focus Across the Firm,* McGraw Hill, New York, pp. 13, 139.

Zeithaml, V.A., Berry L.L. and Parasuraman, A. (1991), "The Nature and Determinants of Customer Expectations of Service", *Marketing Science Institute Research Programme Series* (May), Report No. 91-113.

Zeithaml, V.A., Parasuraman, A. and Barry L.L. (1985) "Problems and Strategies in Services Marketing," *Journal of Marketing,* Vol,. 49, Spring pp. 33-46.

Zeithaml, V.A., Parasuraman, A. and Berry, L.L. (1990) *Delivering Quality Service: Balancing Customer Perceptions and Expectations,* New York: Free Press, p. 28.

Index

I

J

K

L

M

N

P

Q

R

S